SOLDIERS

Charles Swenson

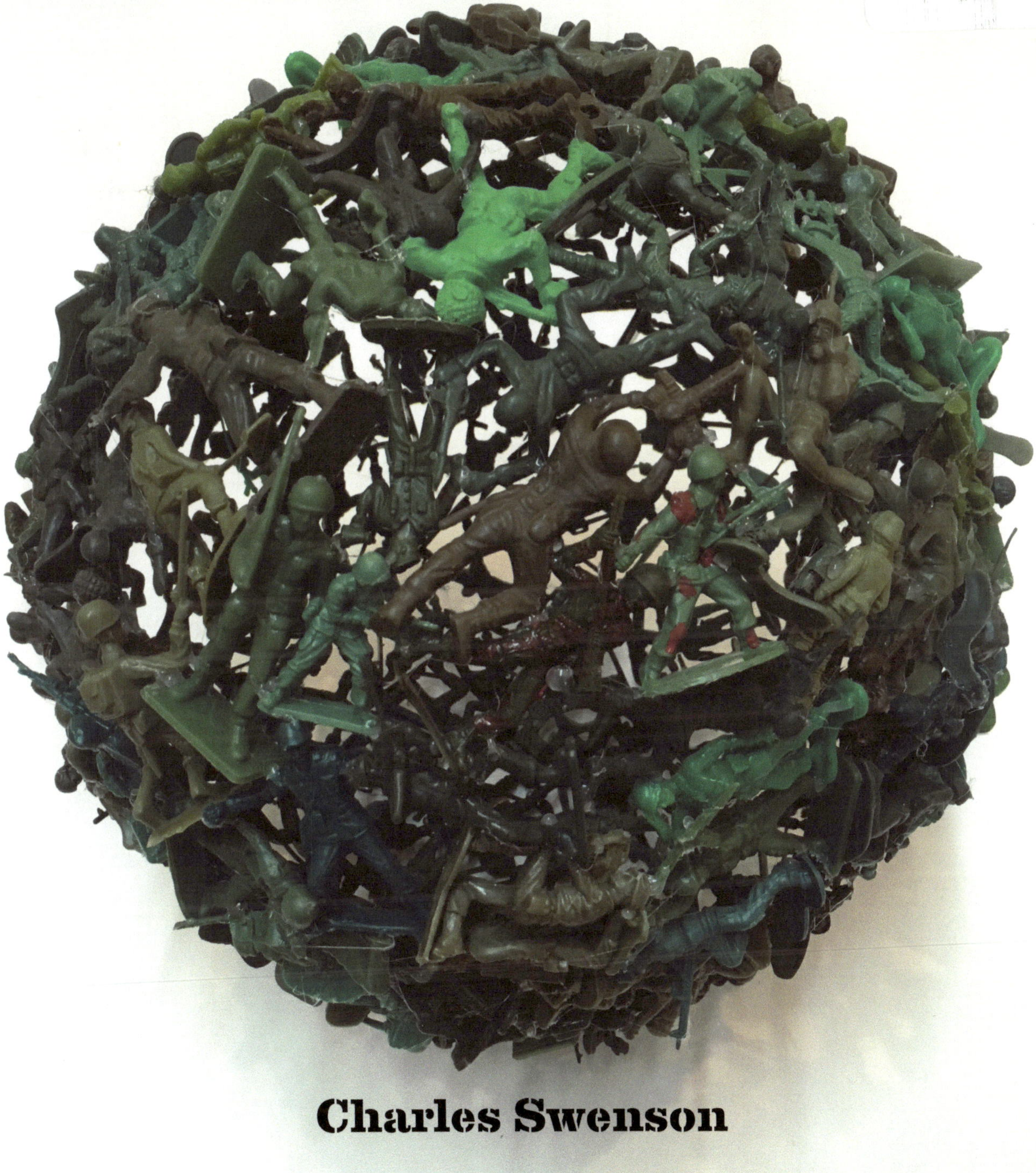

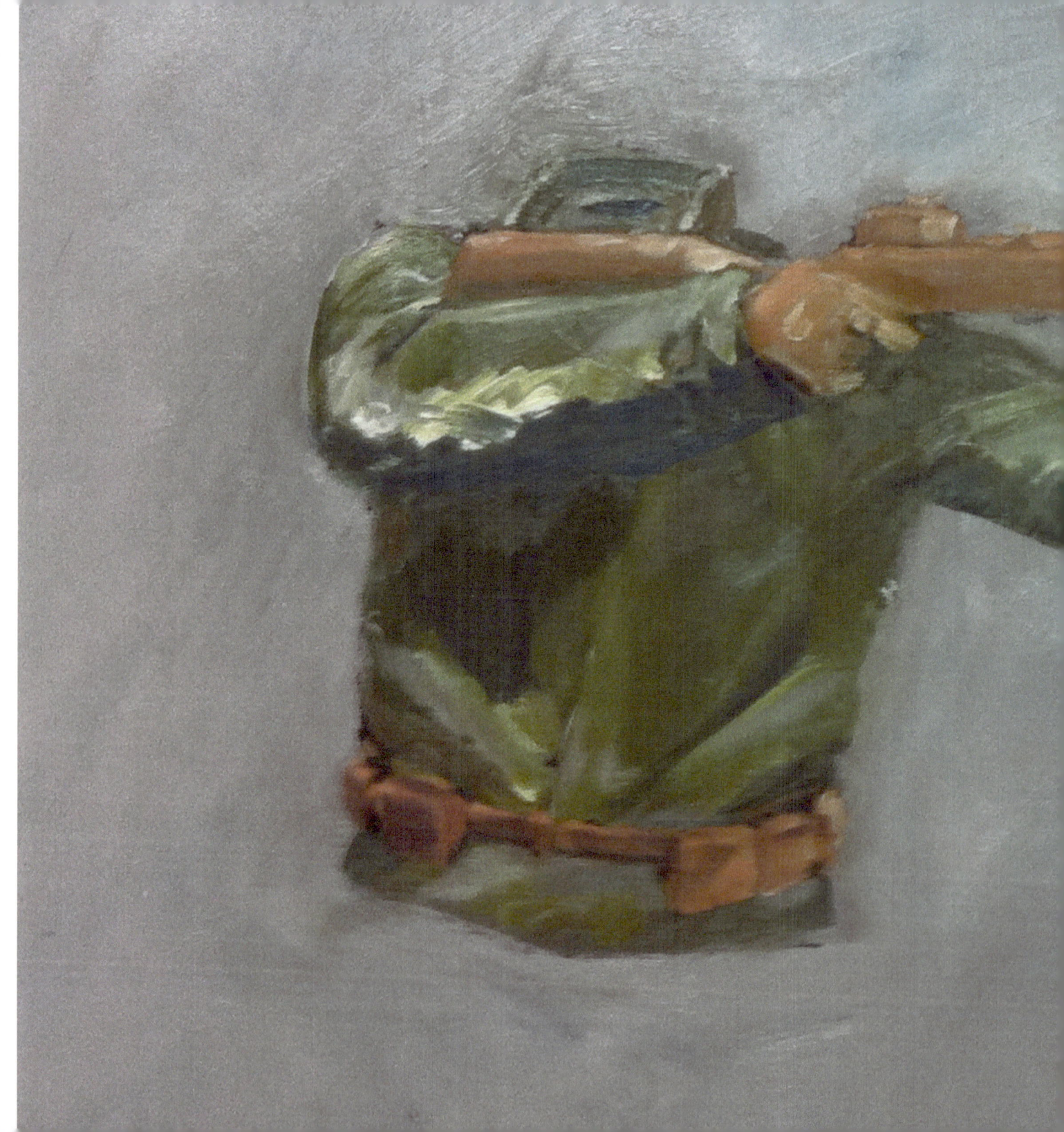

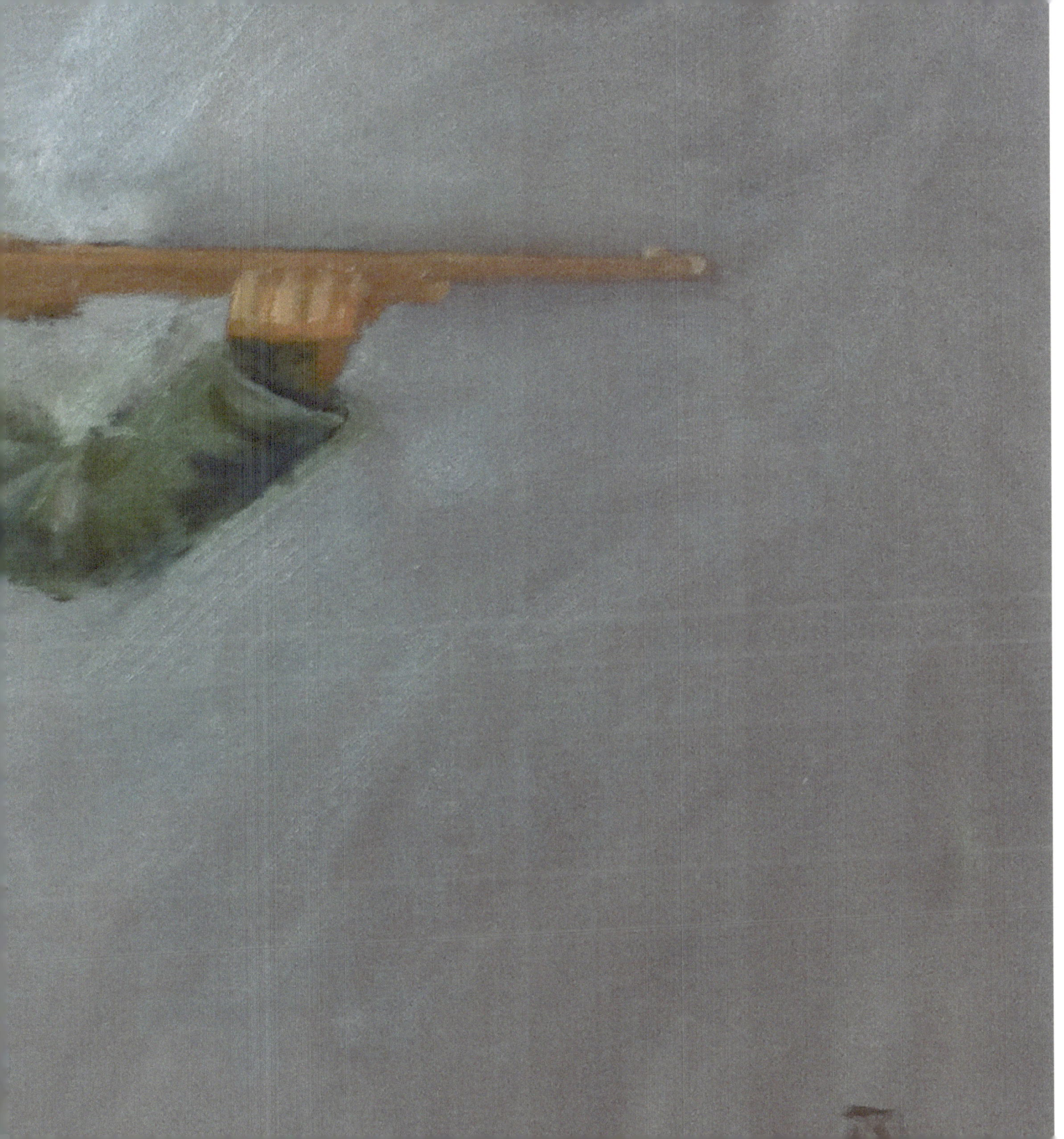

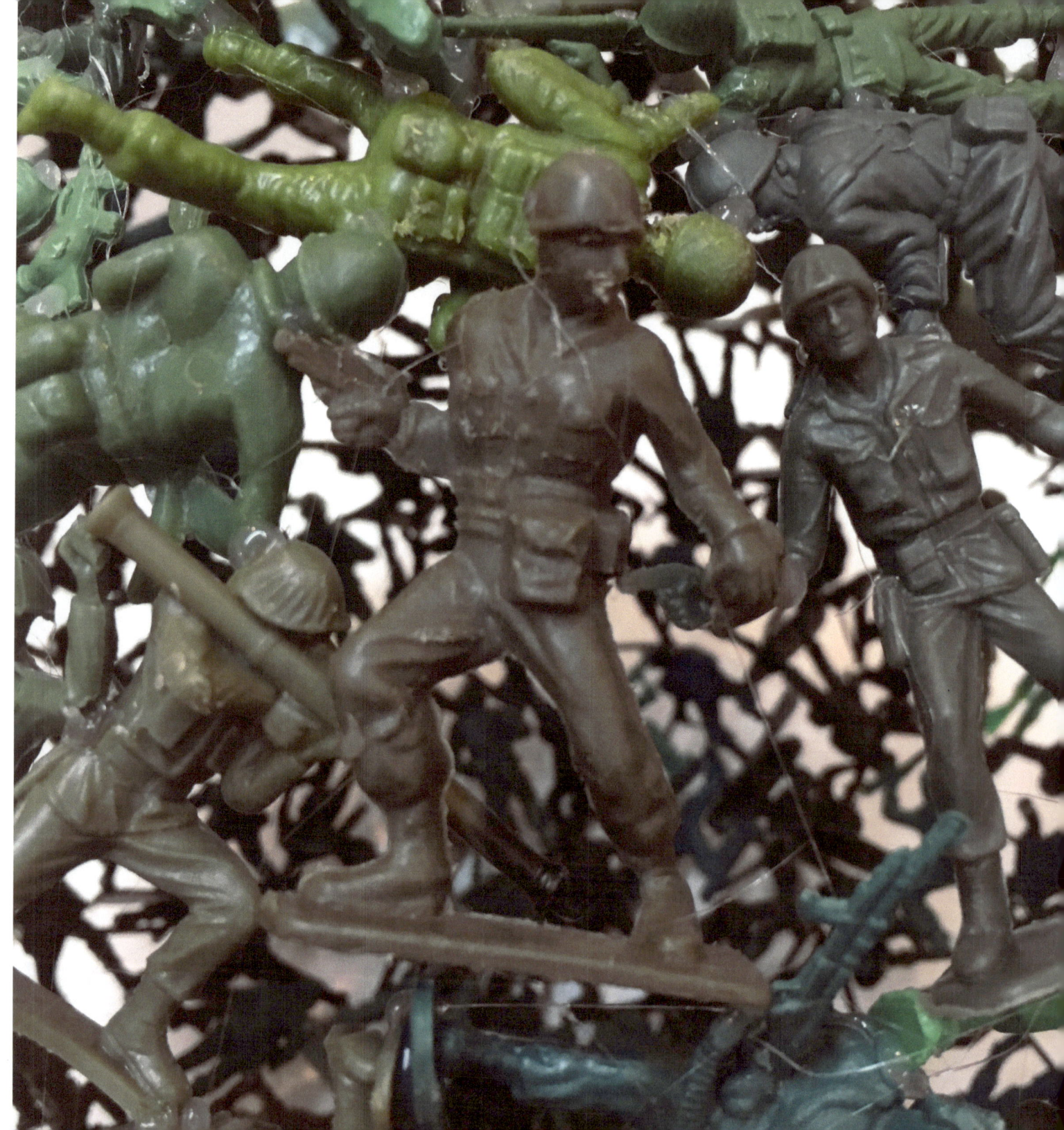

The fragility of the male body is epitomized by the toy soldier. Rendered strong, impervious, brute and proud, this totem is the domain of two distinct sets of males: post toddler boys not yet adolescent controlling the development of their own masculinity and post-mid-life men drenched in sentimentality or pining for control of a memory of once having been free to play.

Charles Swenson paints portraits of toy soldiers, "army men" as many kids call them. The injection-molded plastic makes for blurry faces but the artist magnifies these and paints the blurred flaws and lumpy surfaces to render portraits of every soldier in one. The strength that poses as ready for battle reveals the vulnerability underneath, a feeling that only a soldier knows his self.

The masculine, then, is the subject thru which these portraits are filtered. How does our individual relationship to the concept of the masculine manifest in our psyches when we see a portrait of one soldier that is every soldier. So much is asked of the soldier, so much is expected and yet the archetype of the soldier is so limited, so subservient to orders. Even the women who serve their countries take on new layers of subservience in this role. Literature asks sympathy for the devil so Charles Swenson insists on at least some empathy for the flesh known as military property.

The artist was once an animator, was always a painter and is presently at work in a spacious art studio looking at magnified faces of plastic memories under the natural light of Downtown Los Angeles. The freedom of childhood to play at will remains within his grasp as long as he is armed with a pencil or paintbrush. The service of many informs the aesthetic of one. In these pools of plastic rendered with oil, the service of the male body is reunited with its soul.

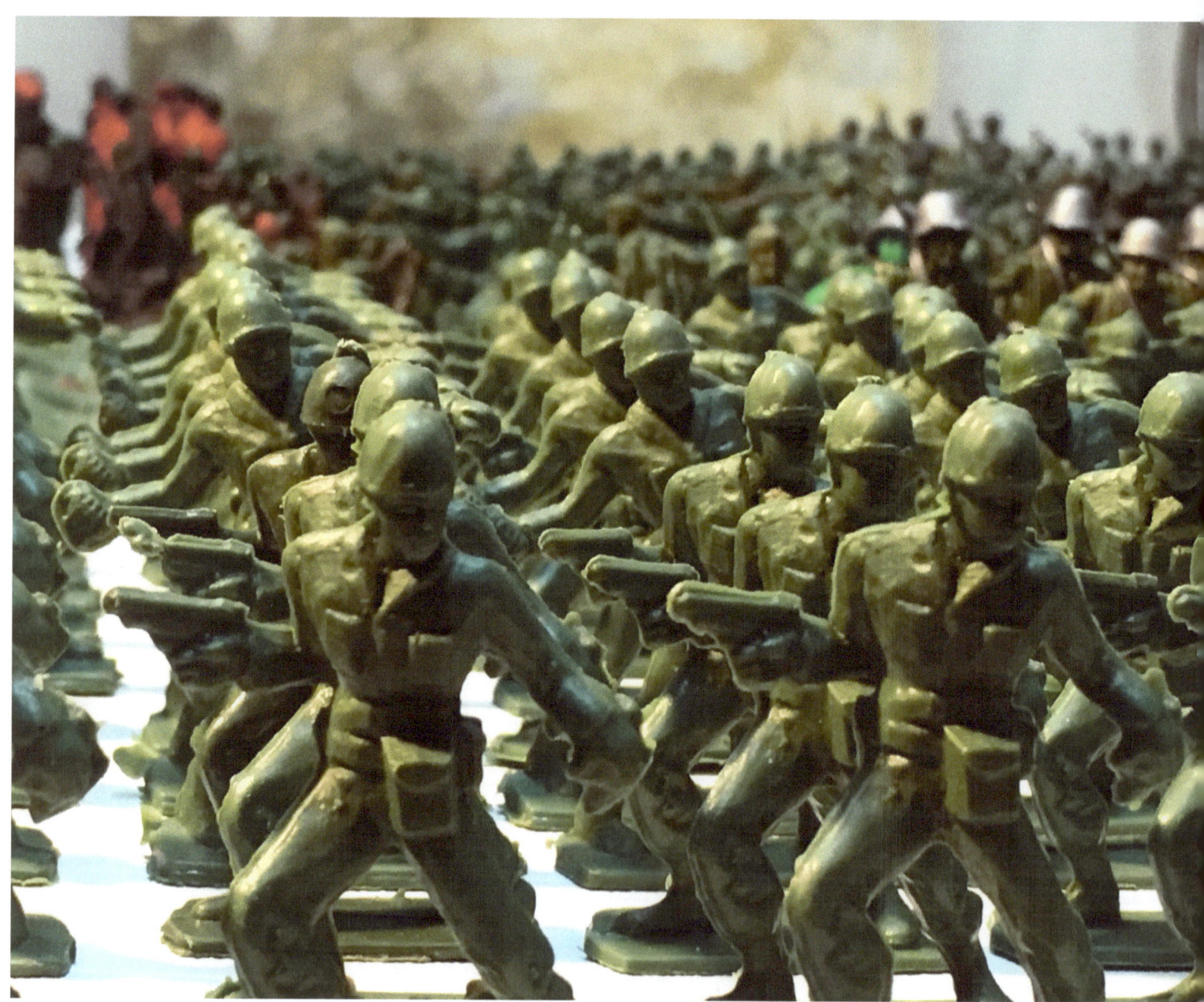

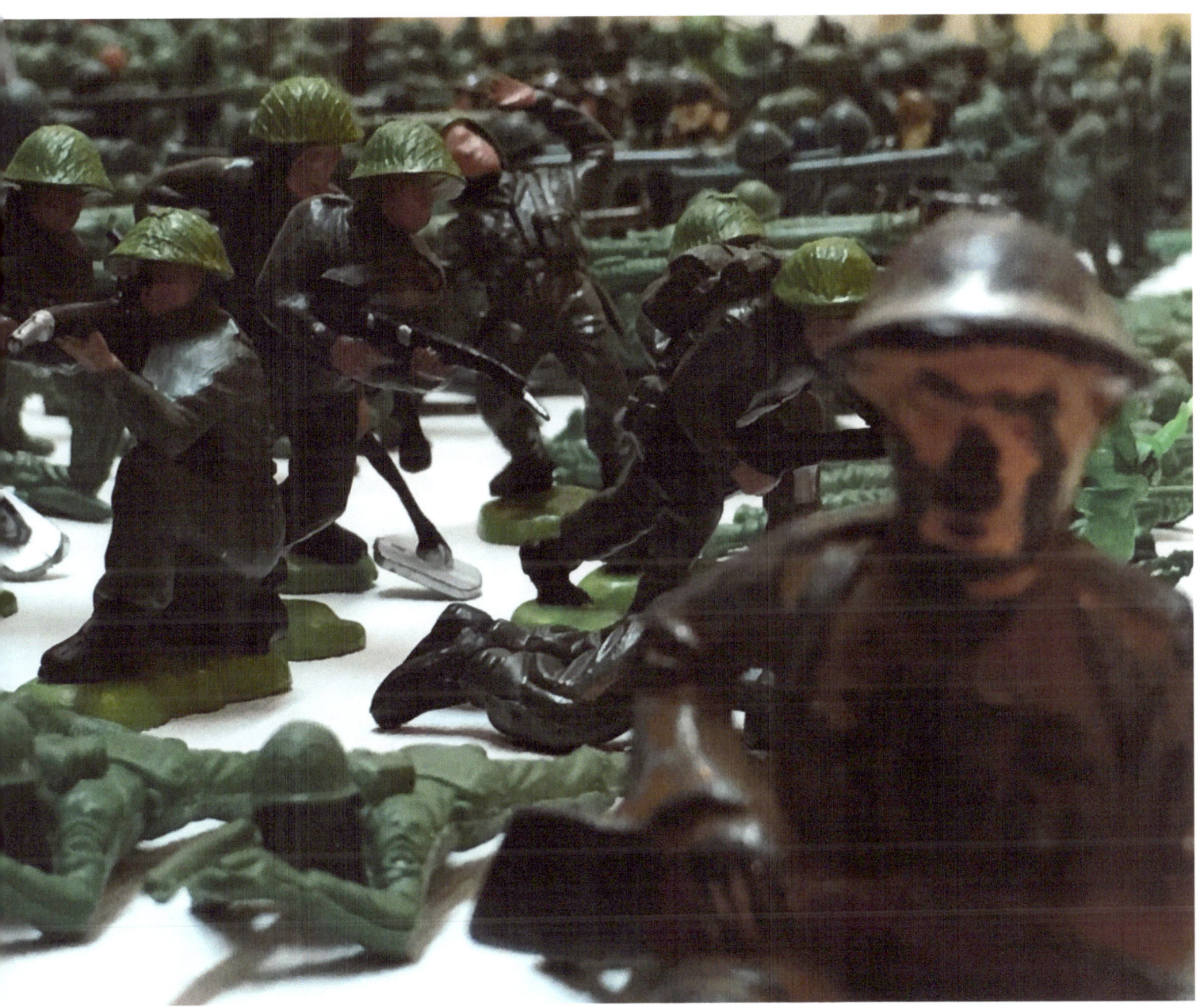

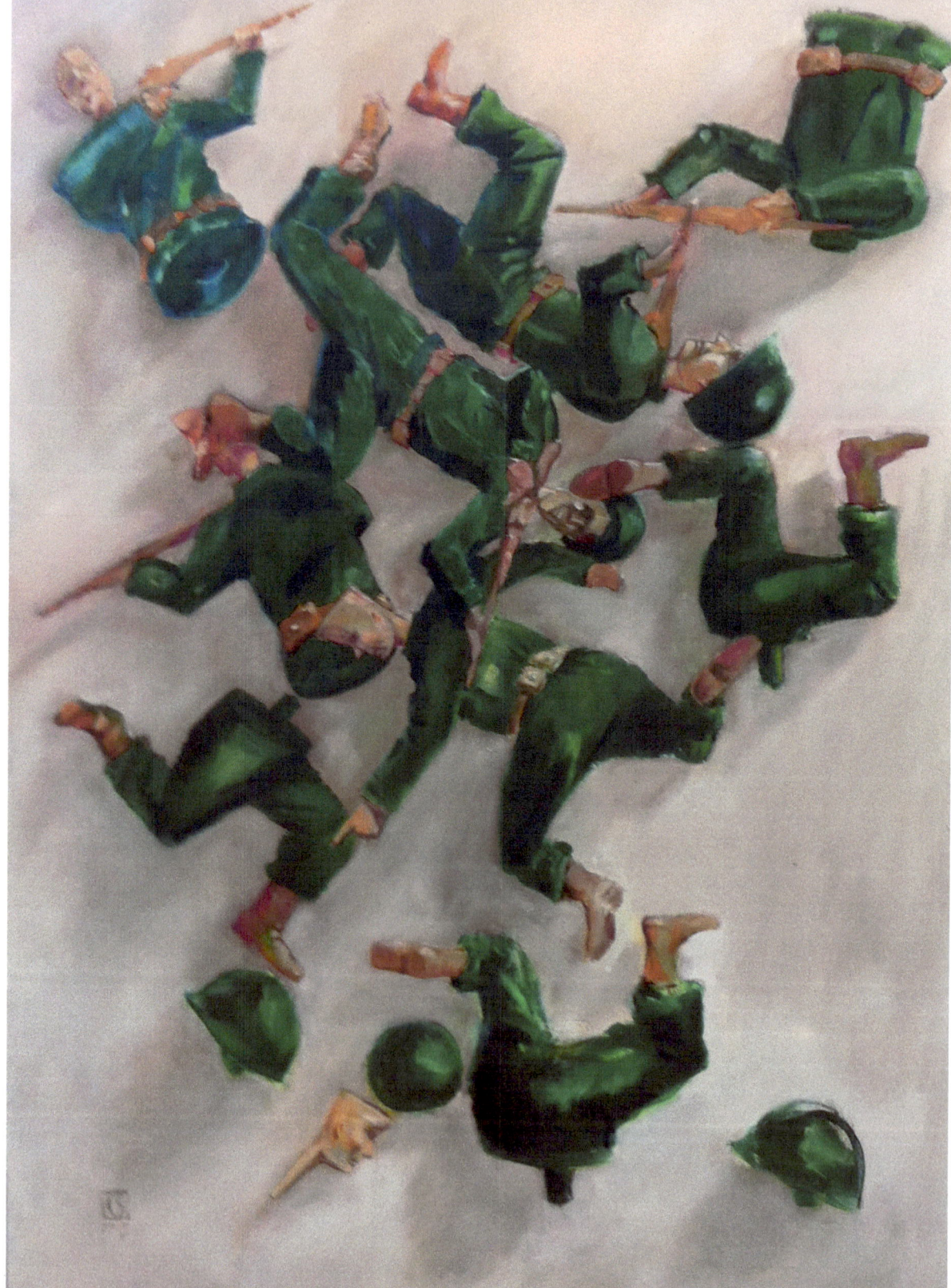

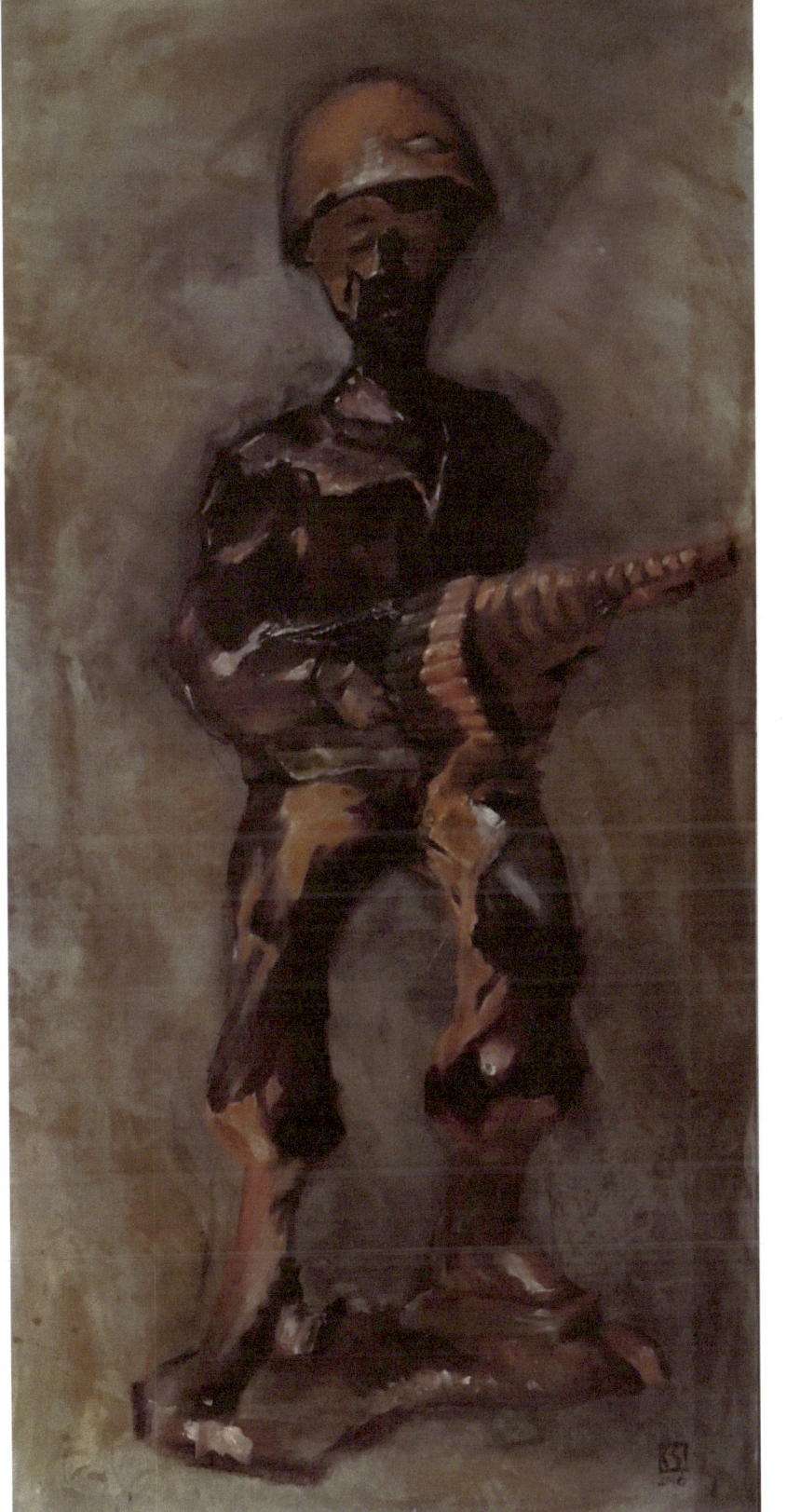

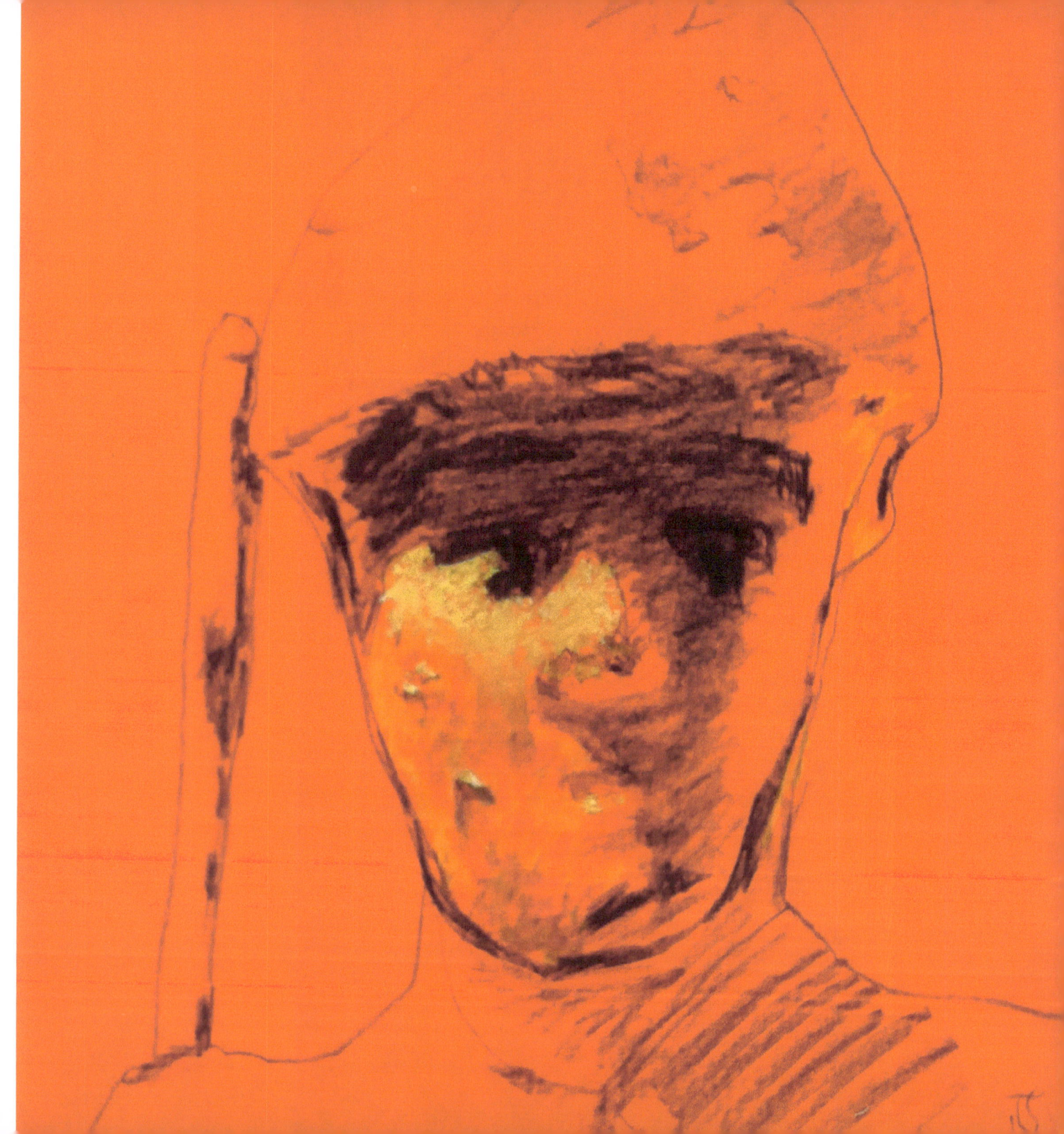

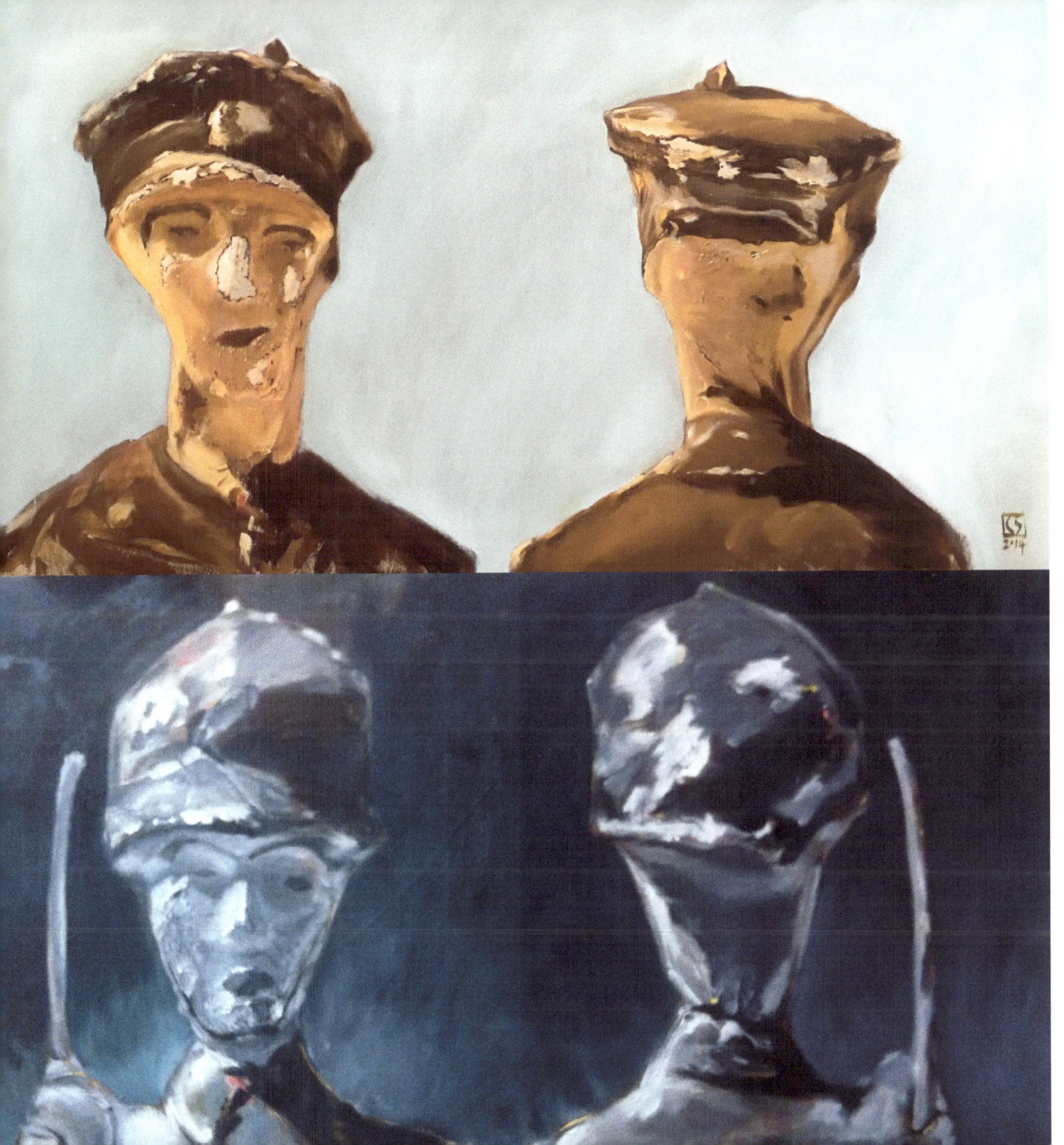

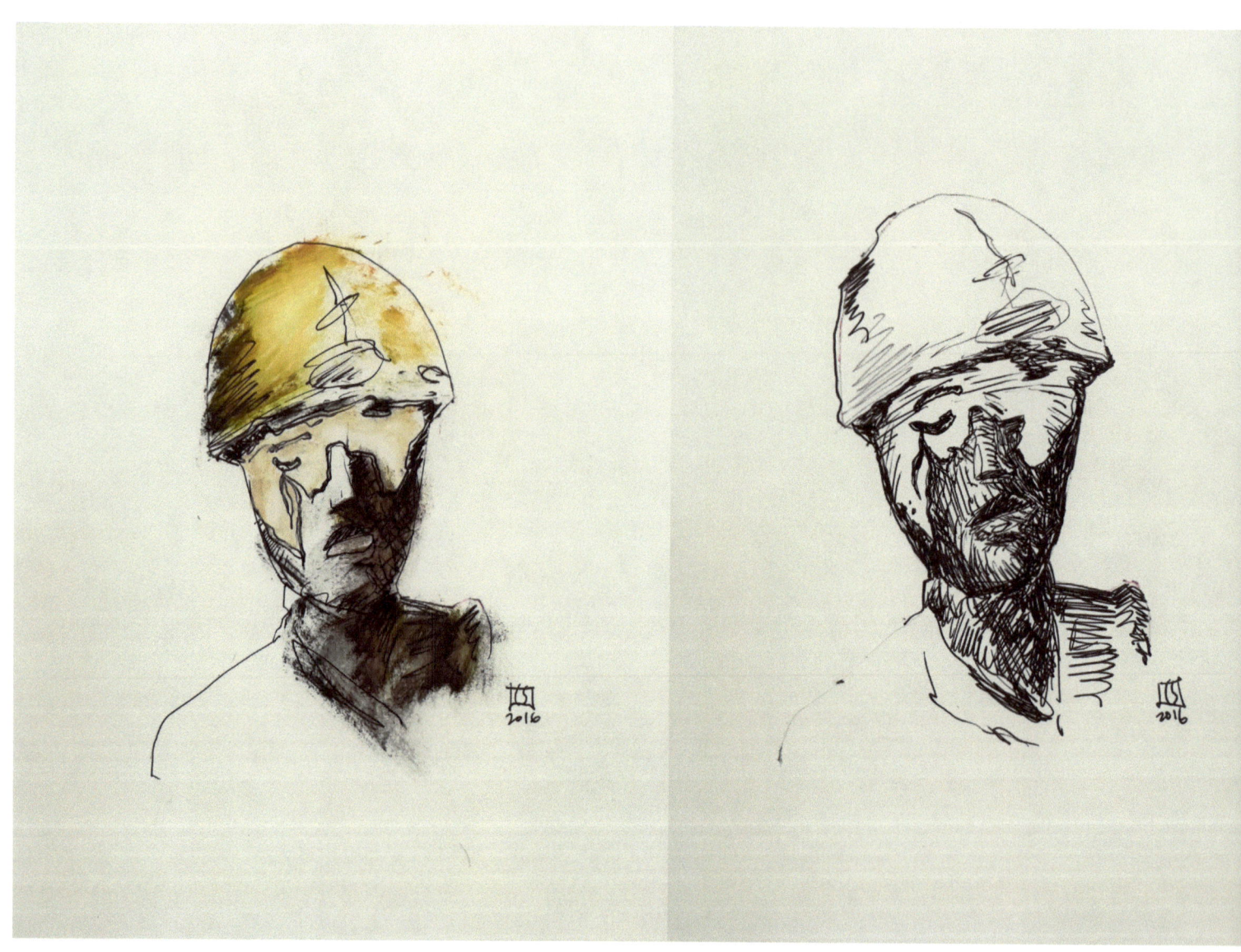

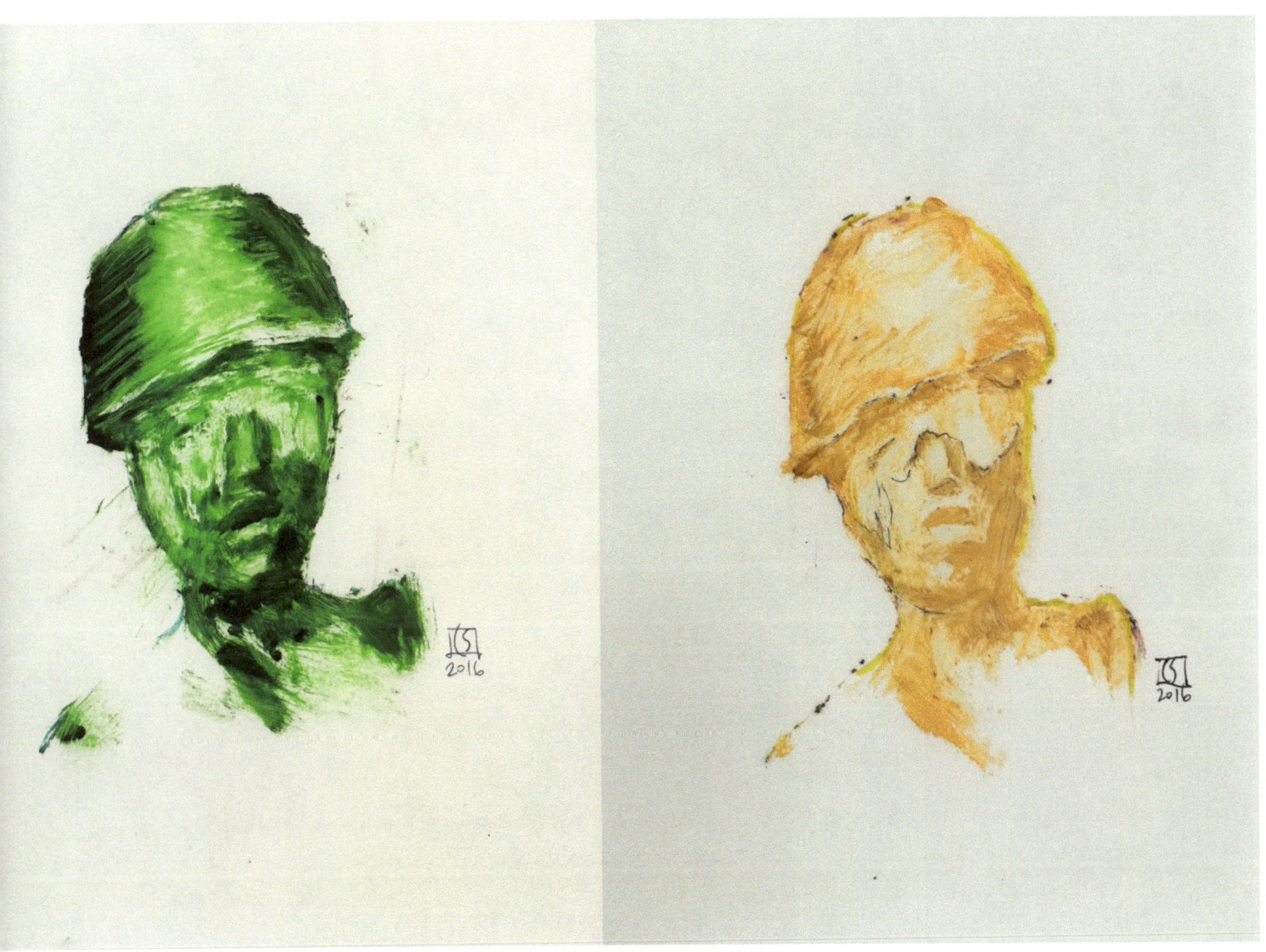

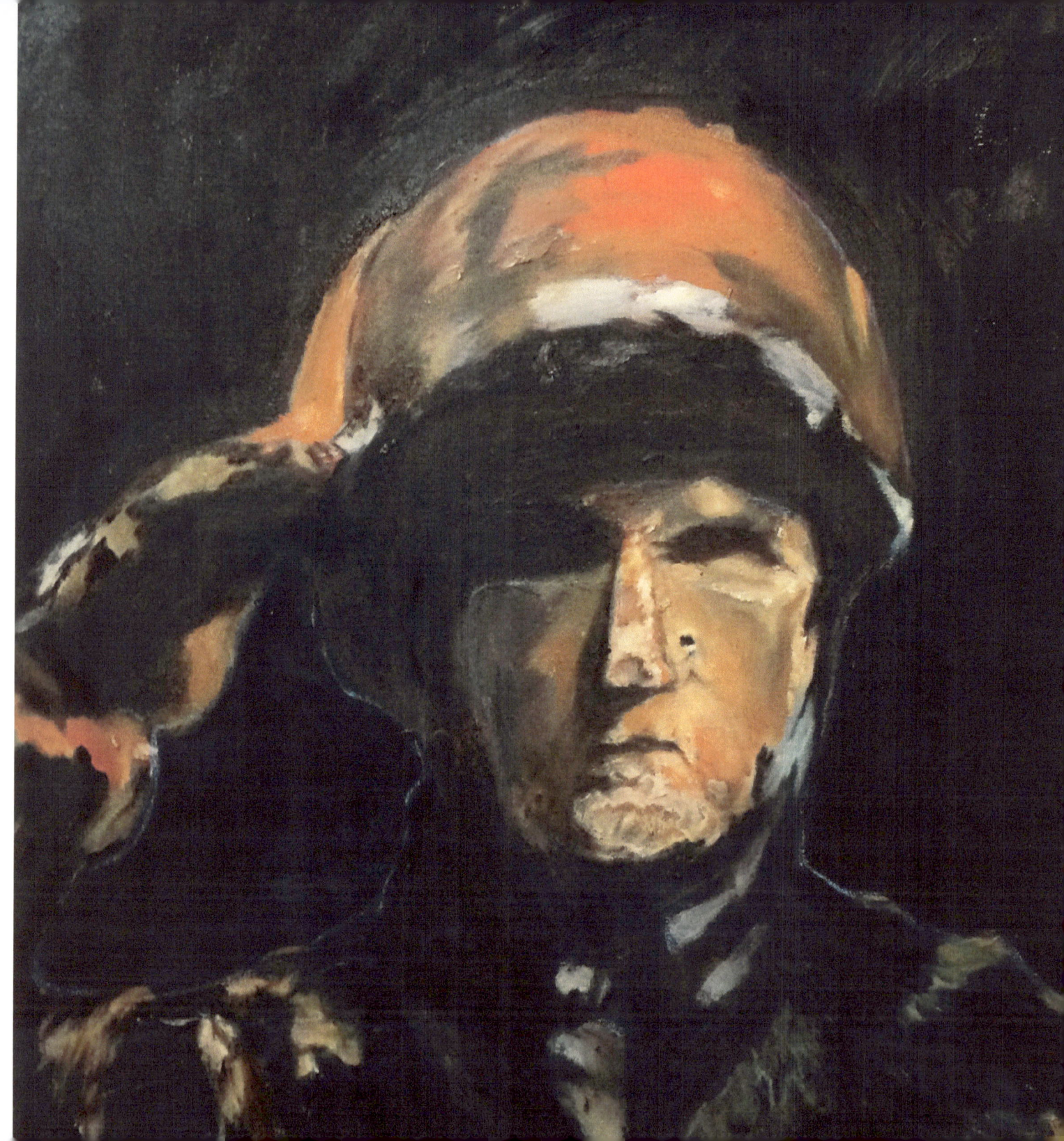

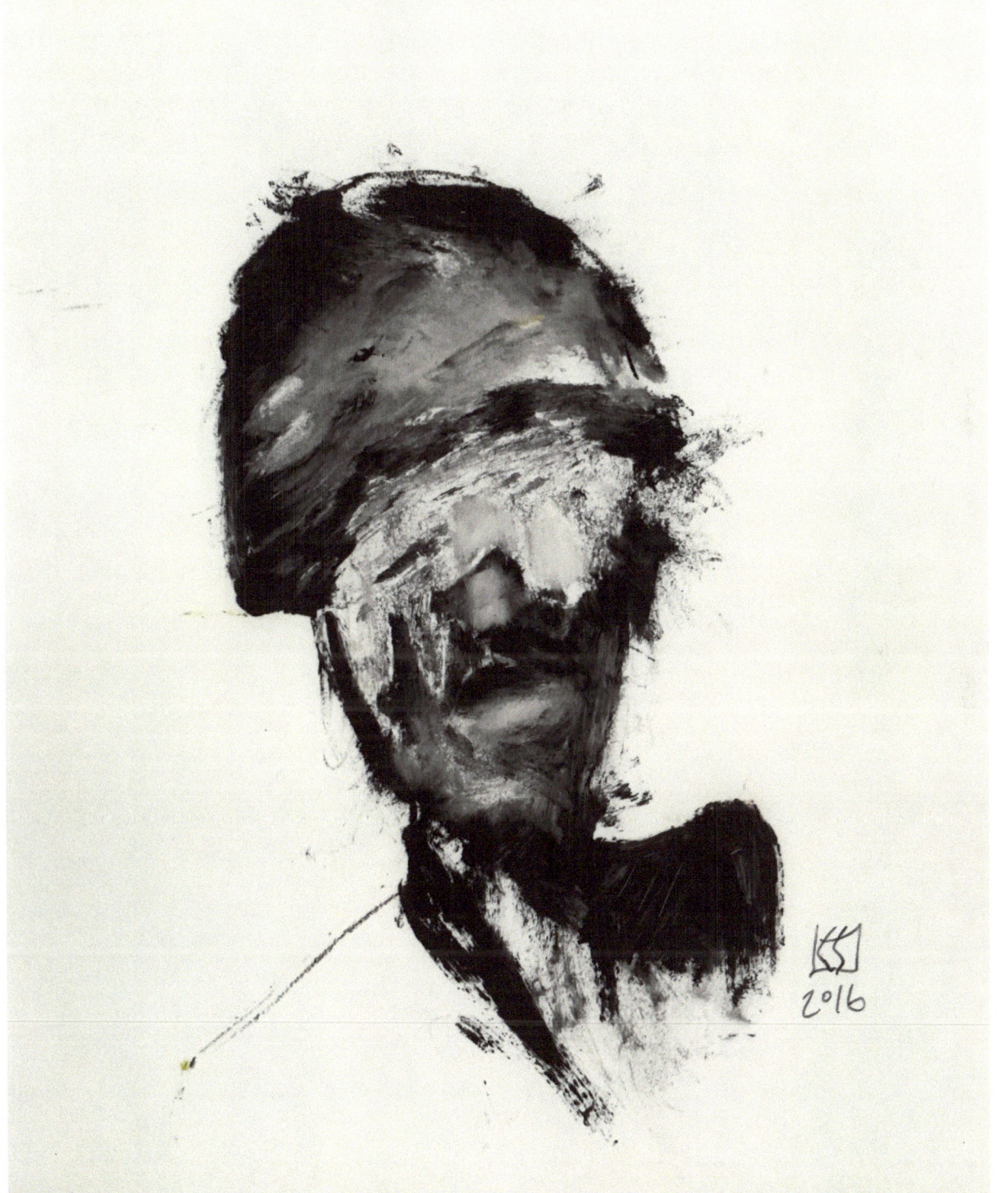

2016

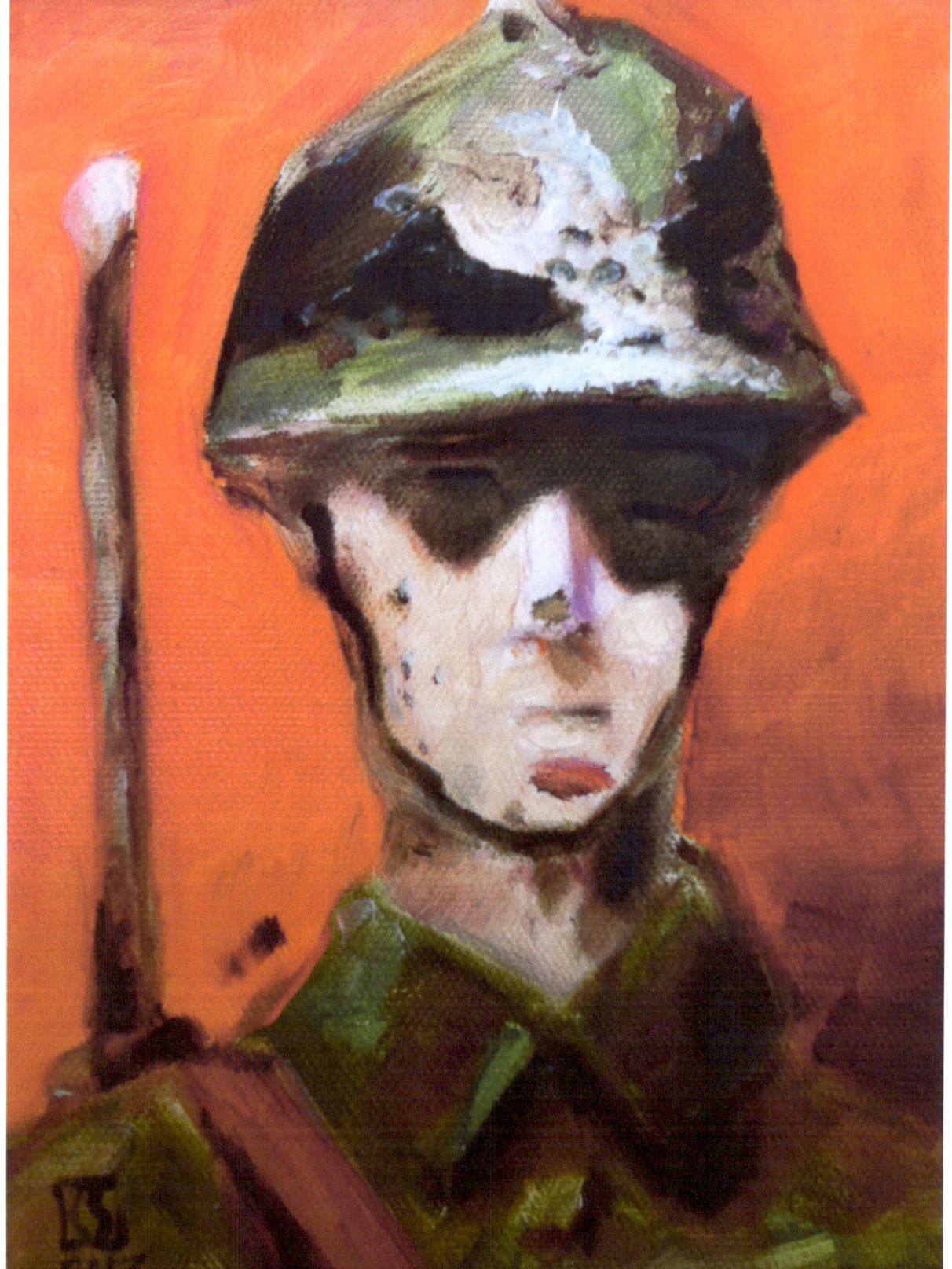

16

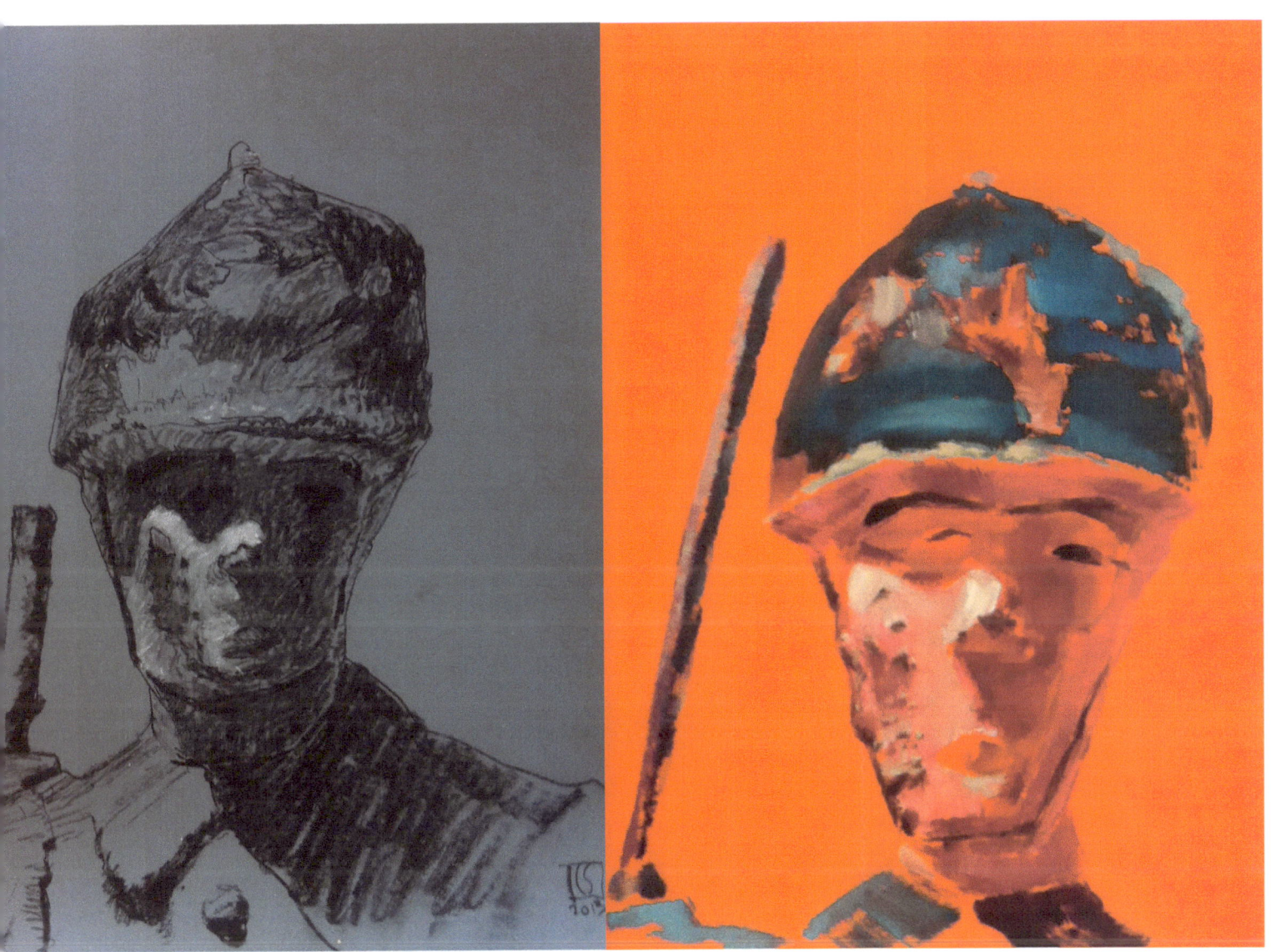

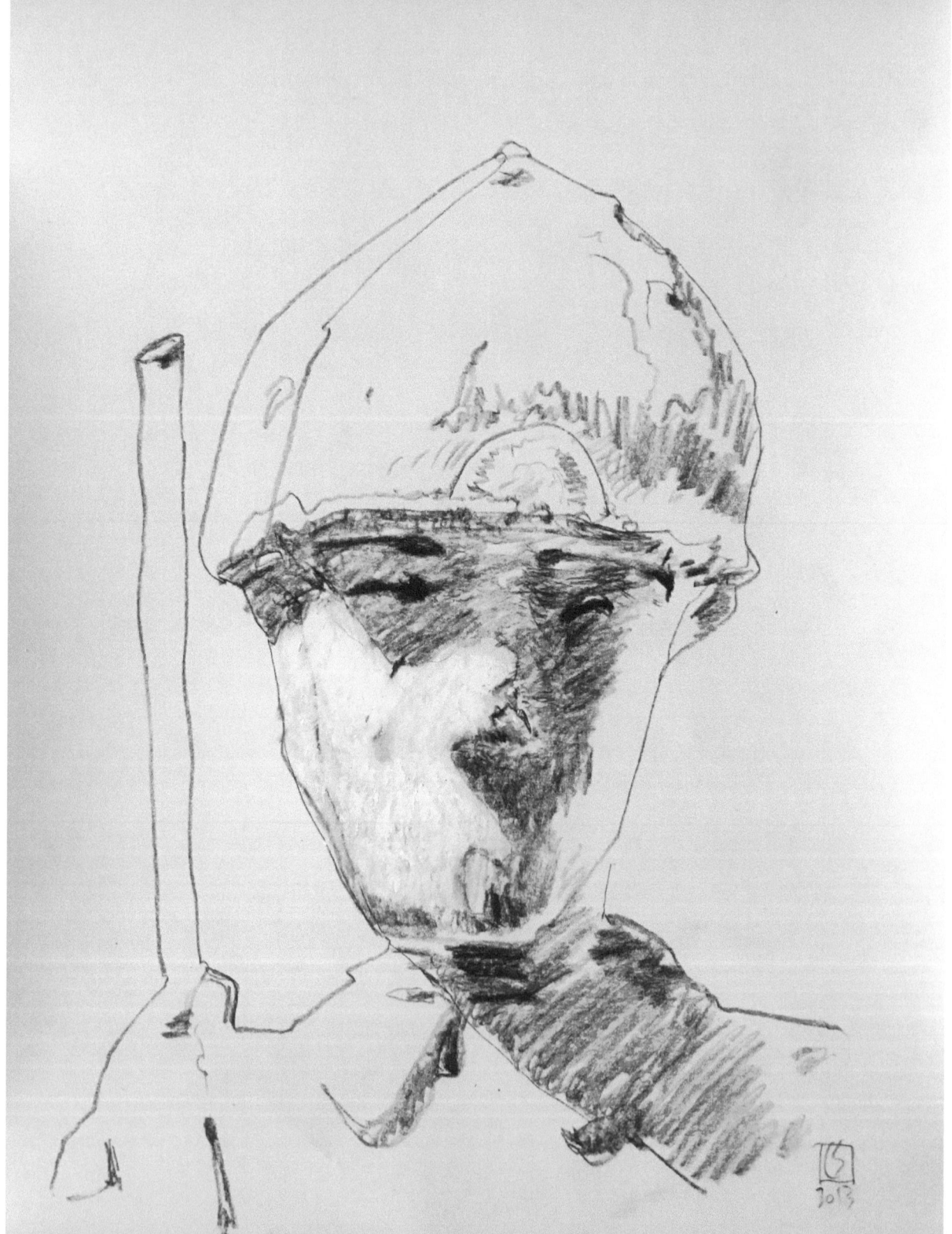

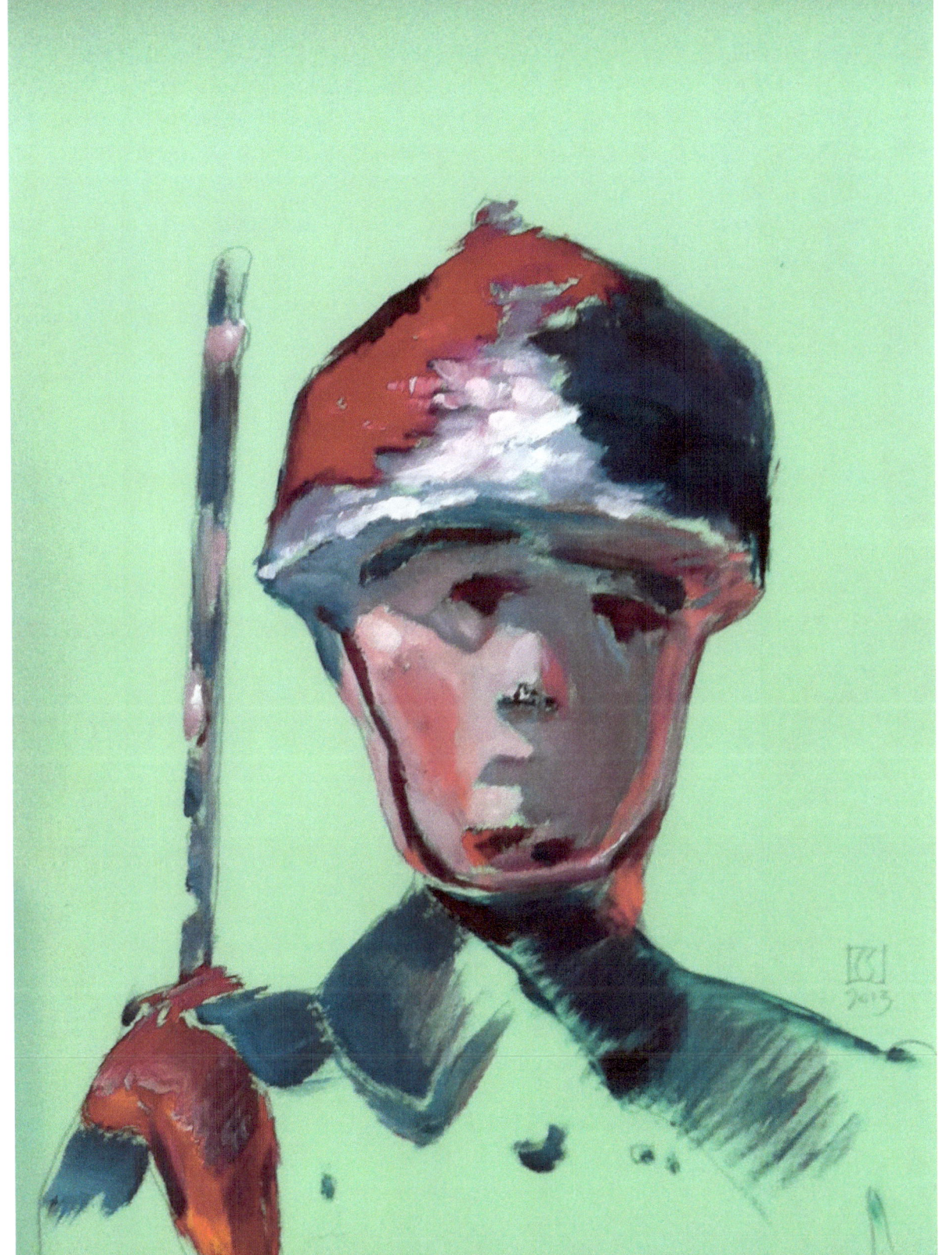

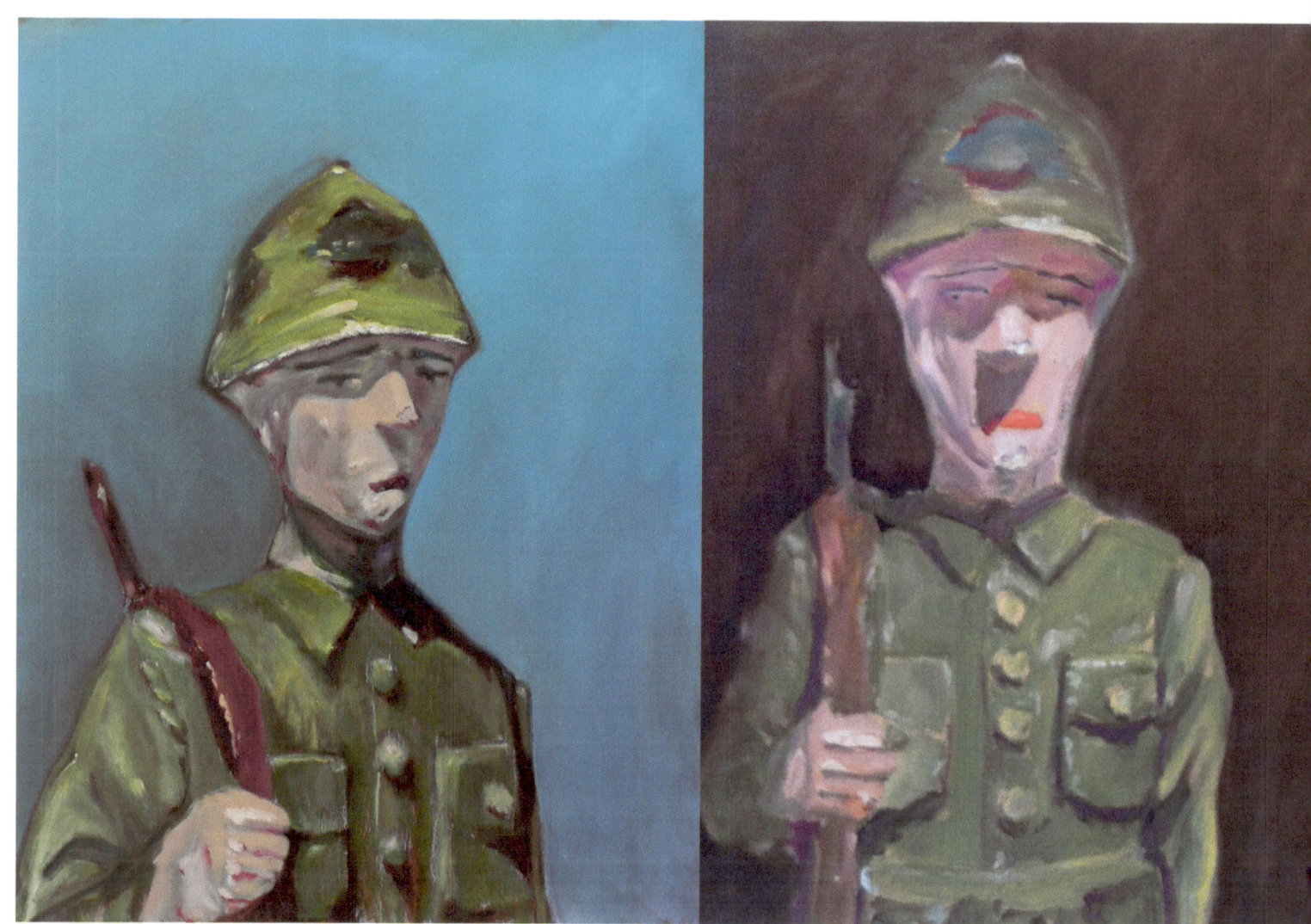

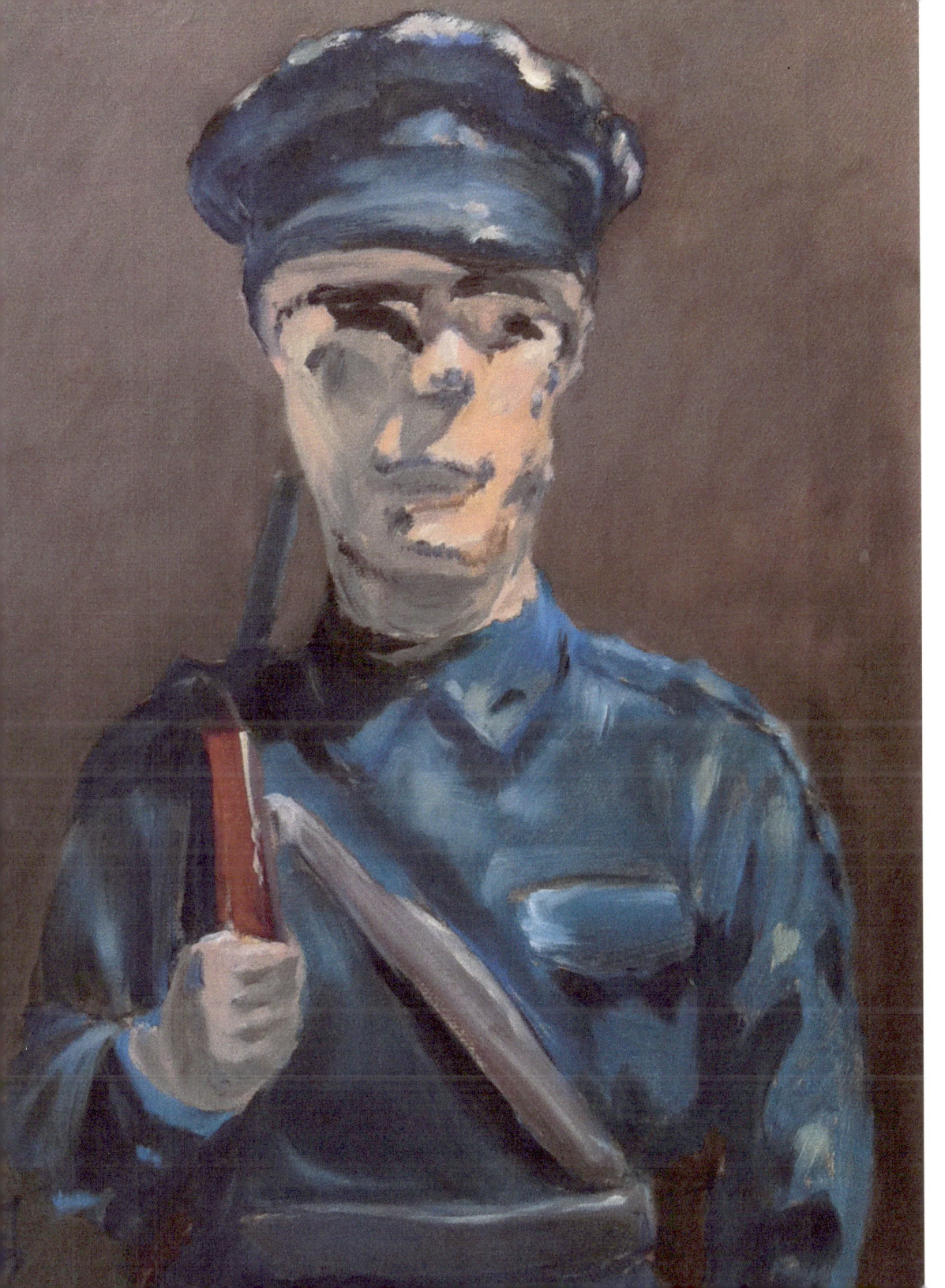

21

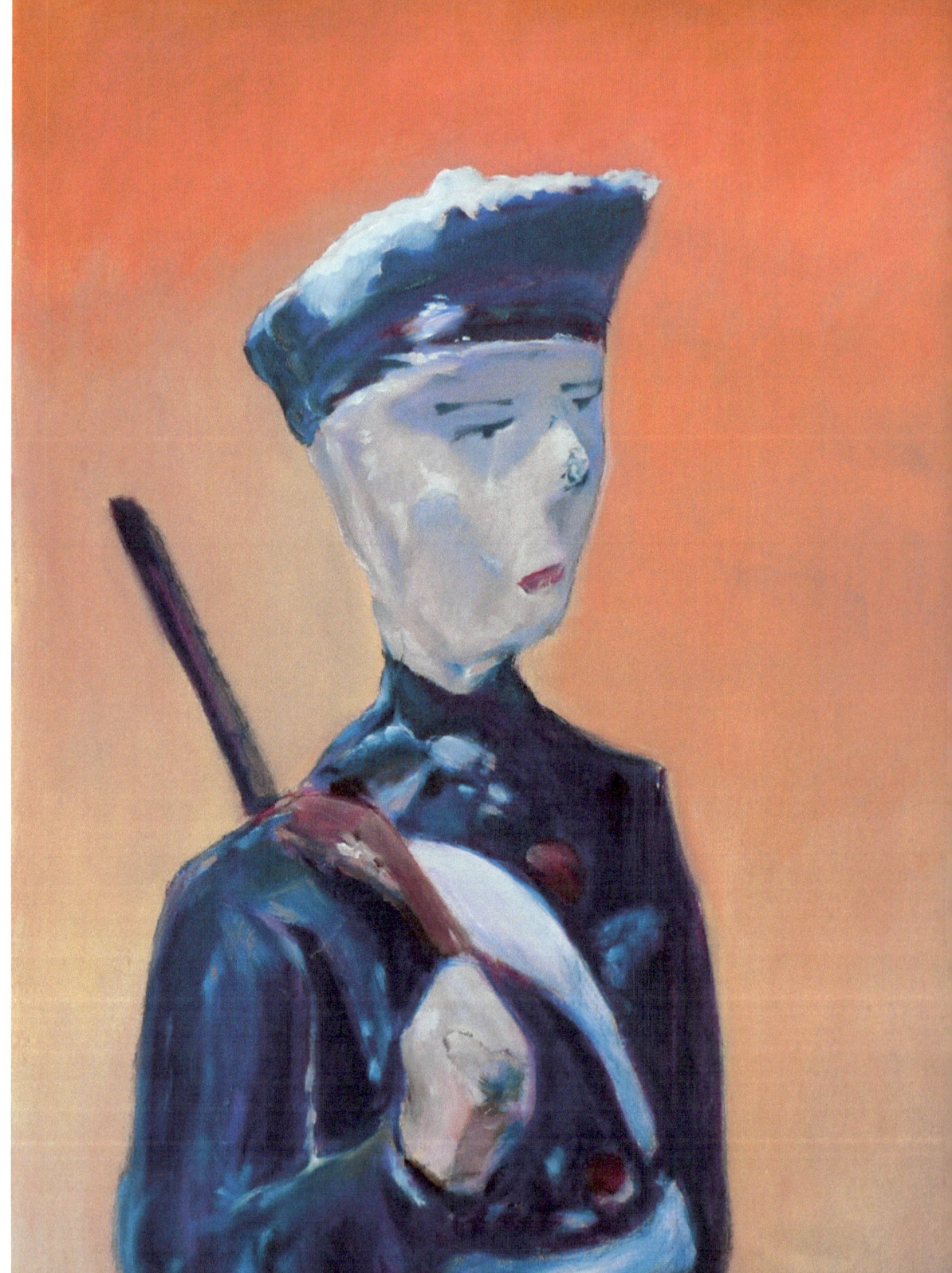

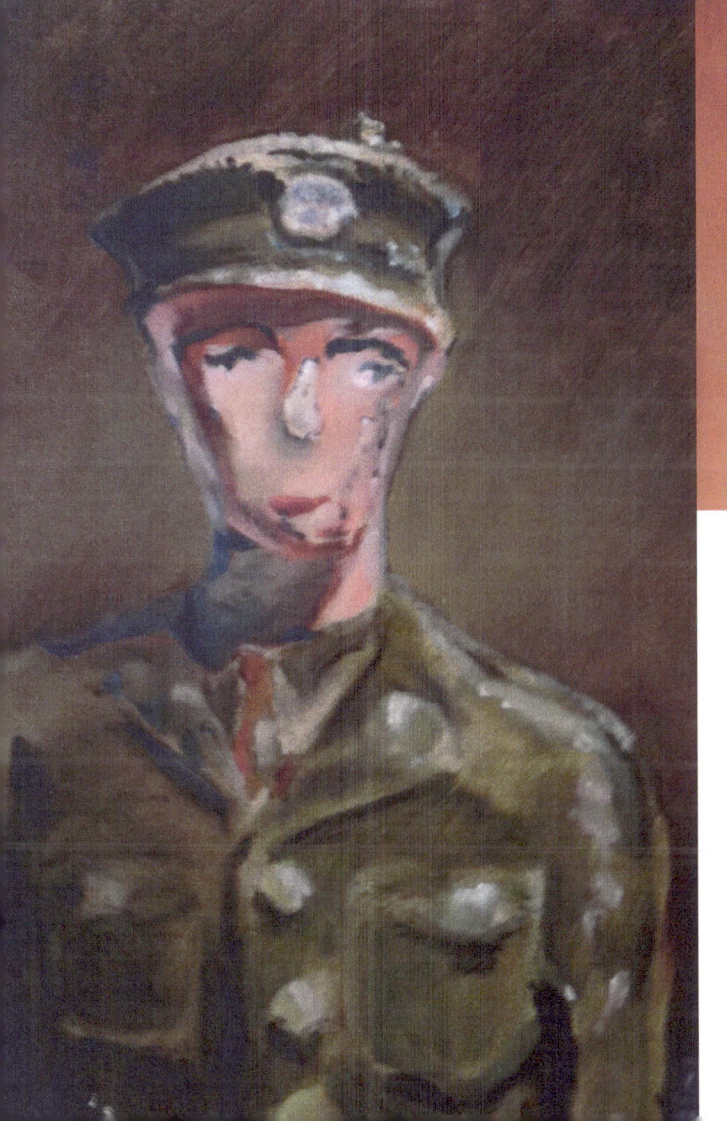

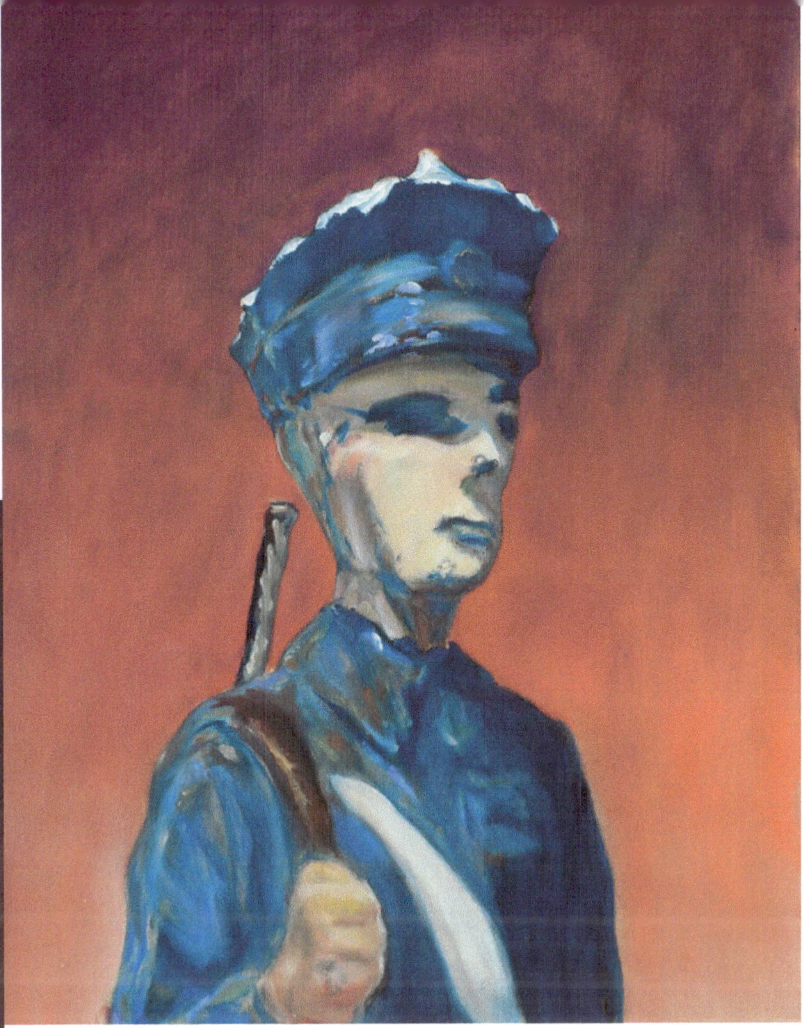

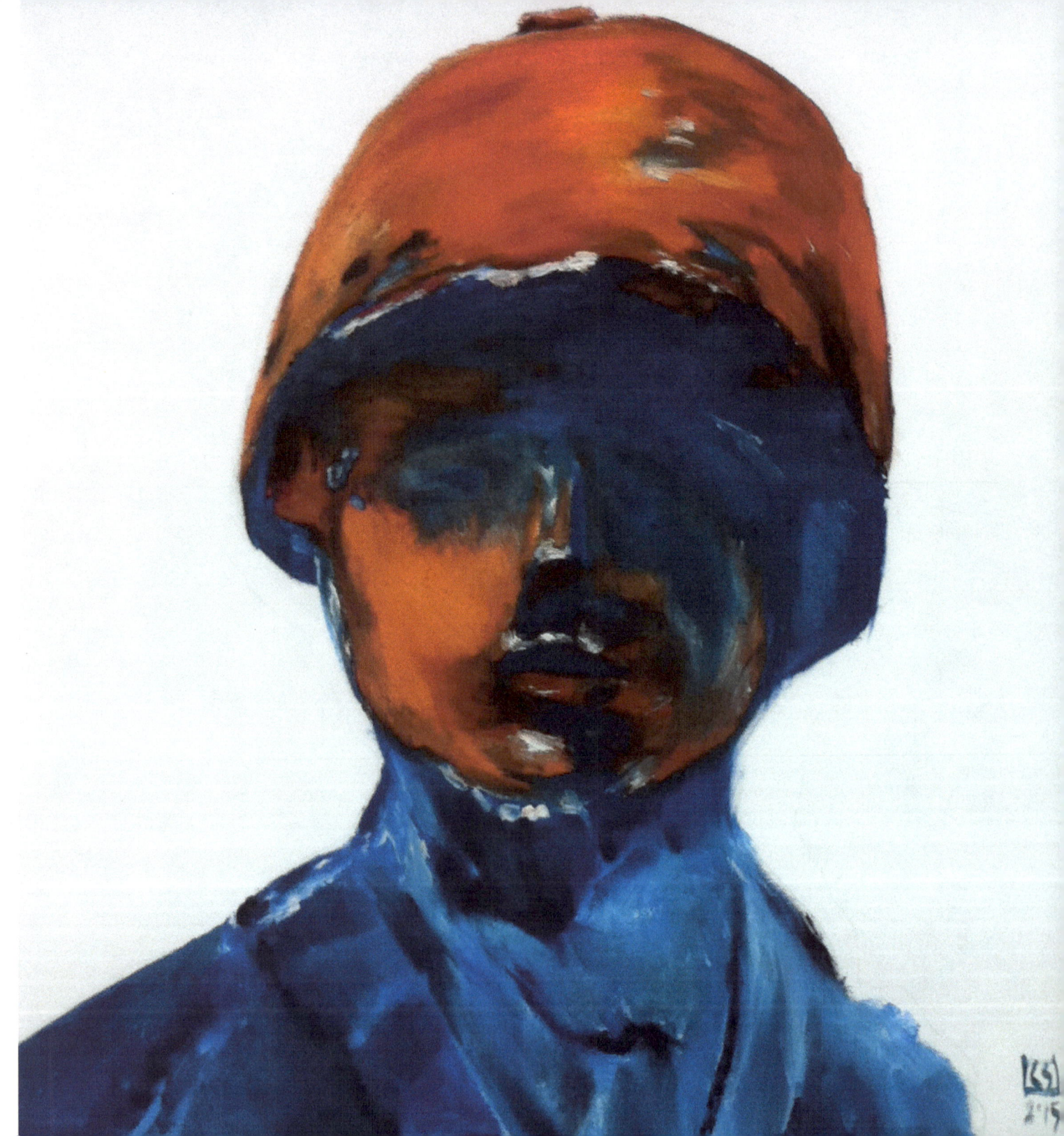

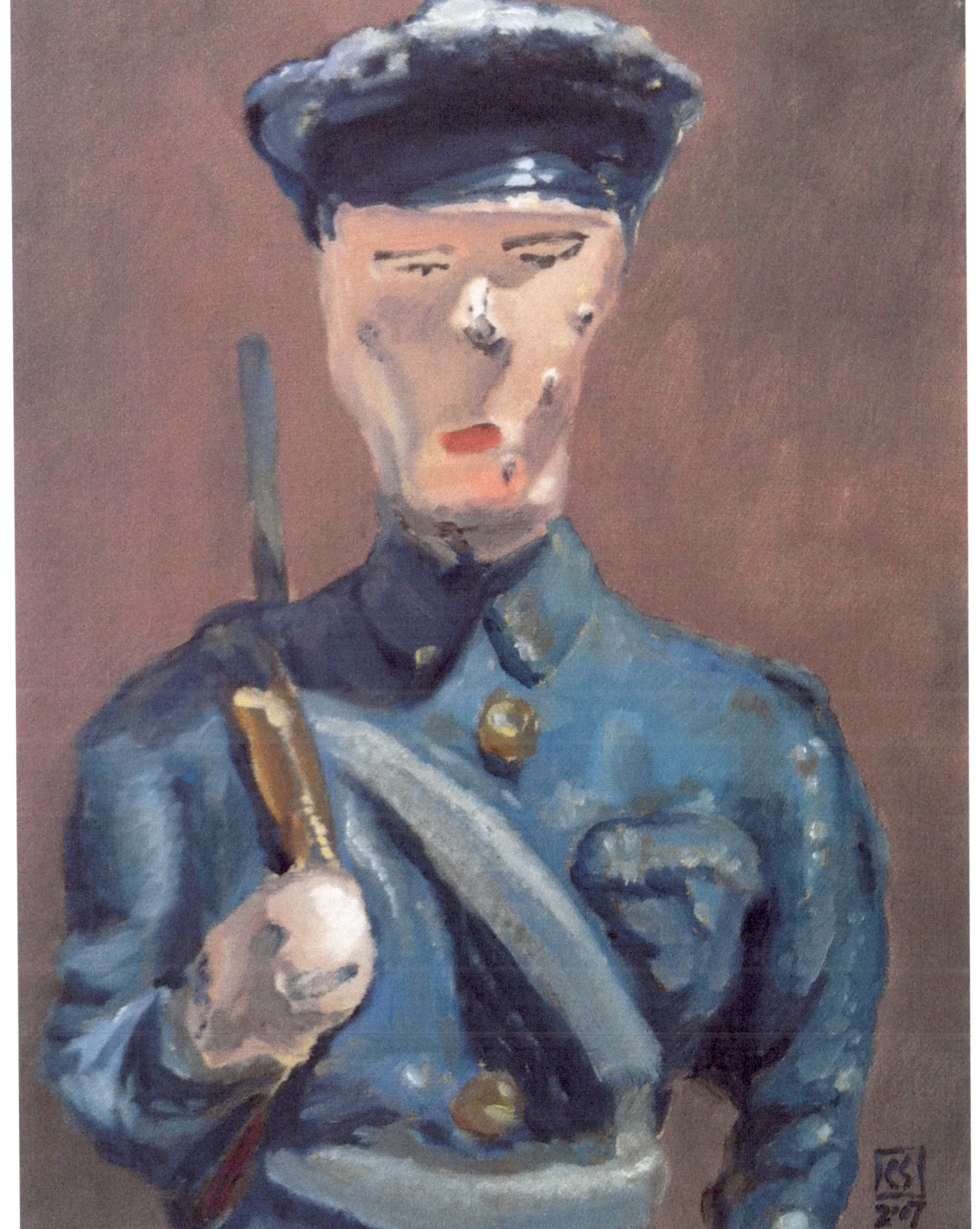

25

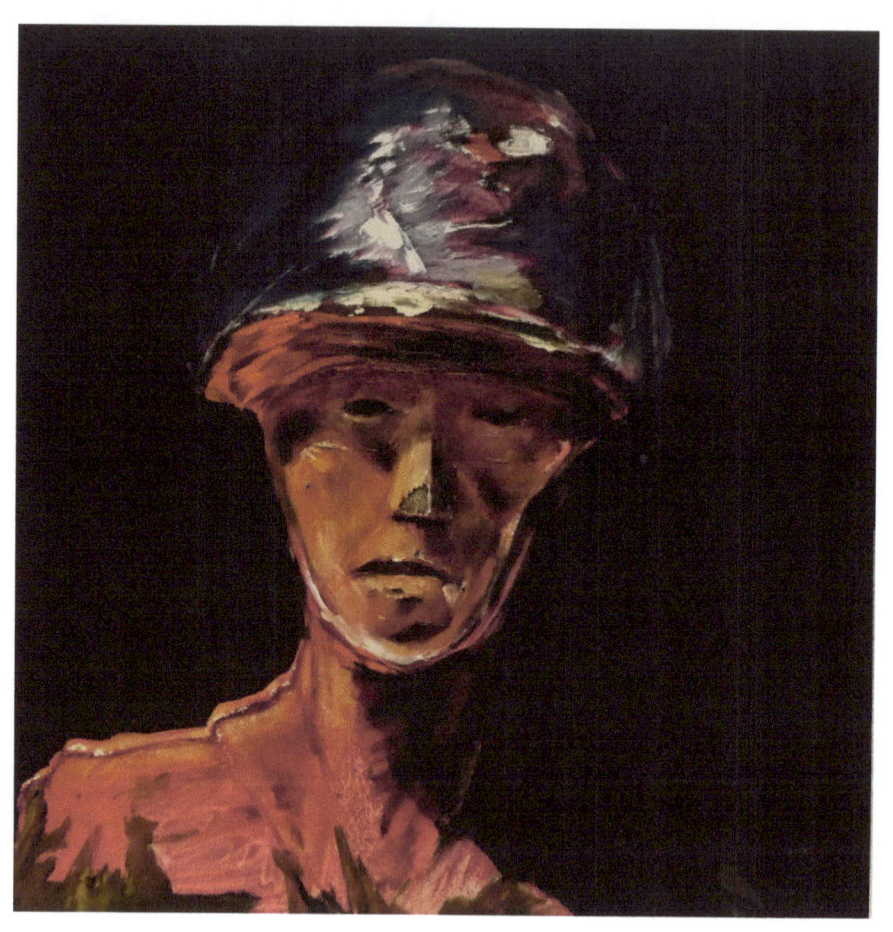

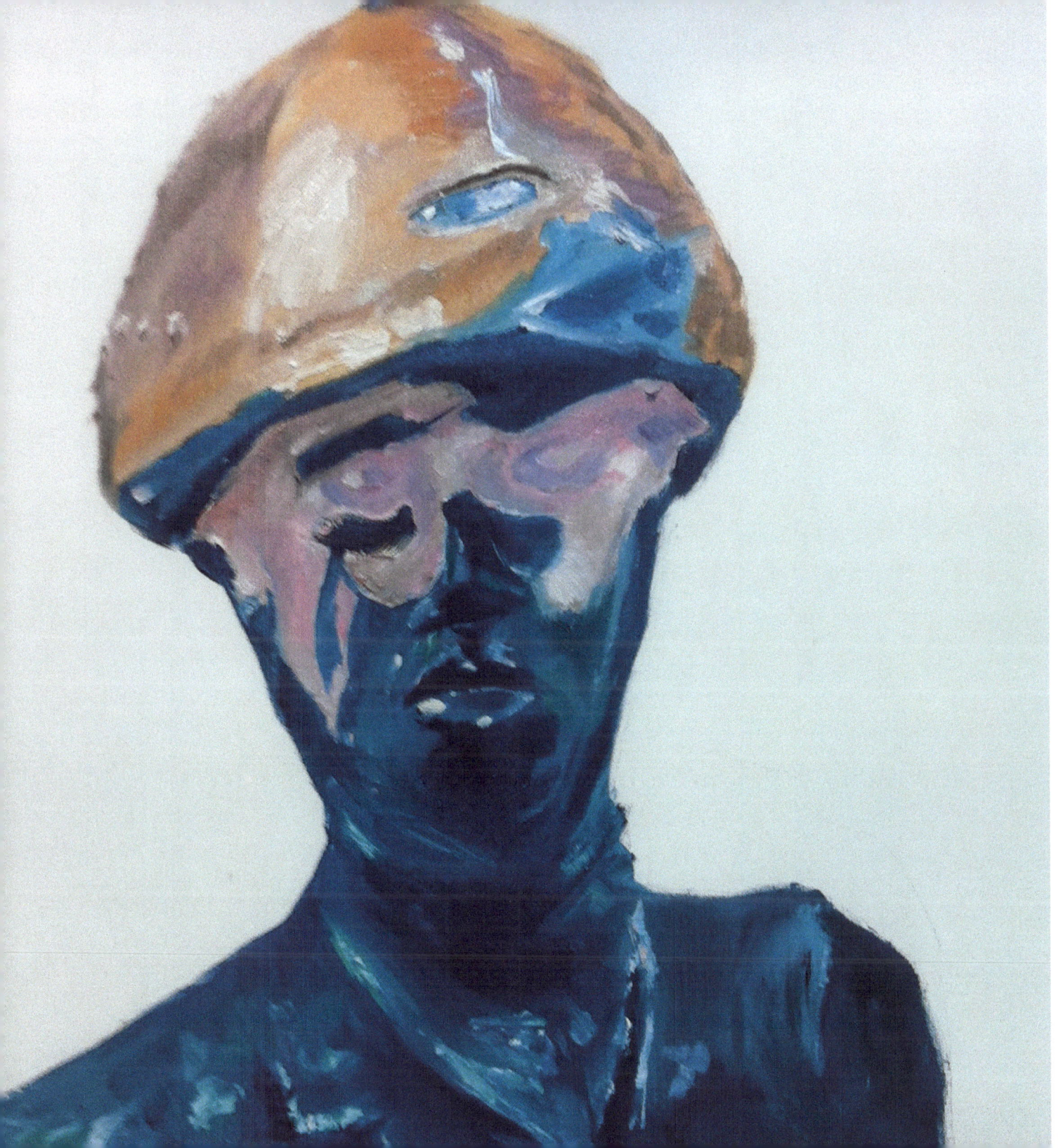

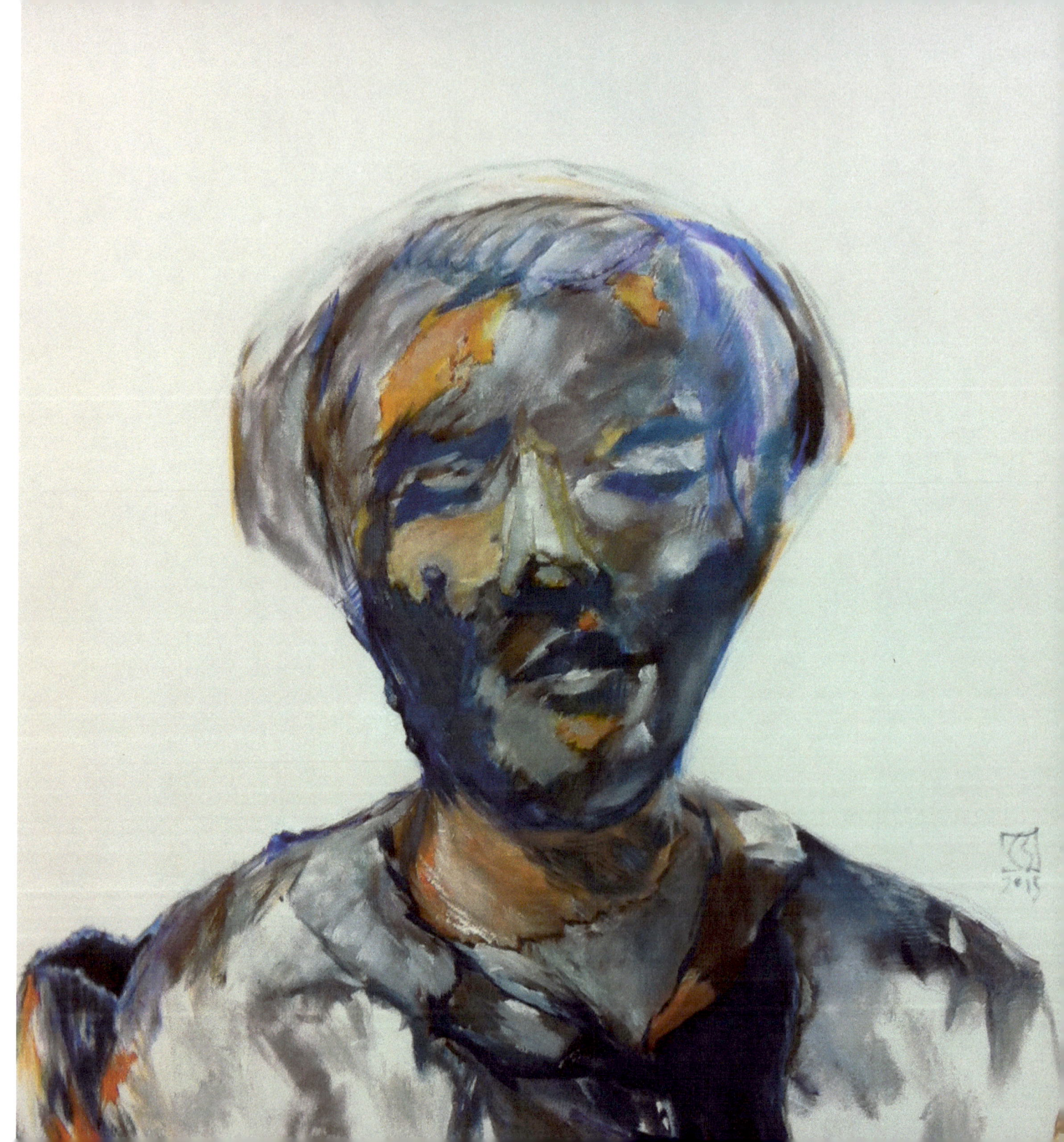

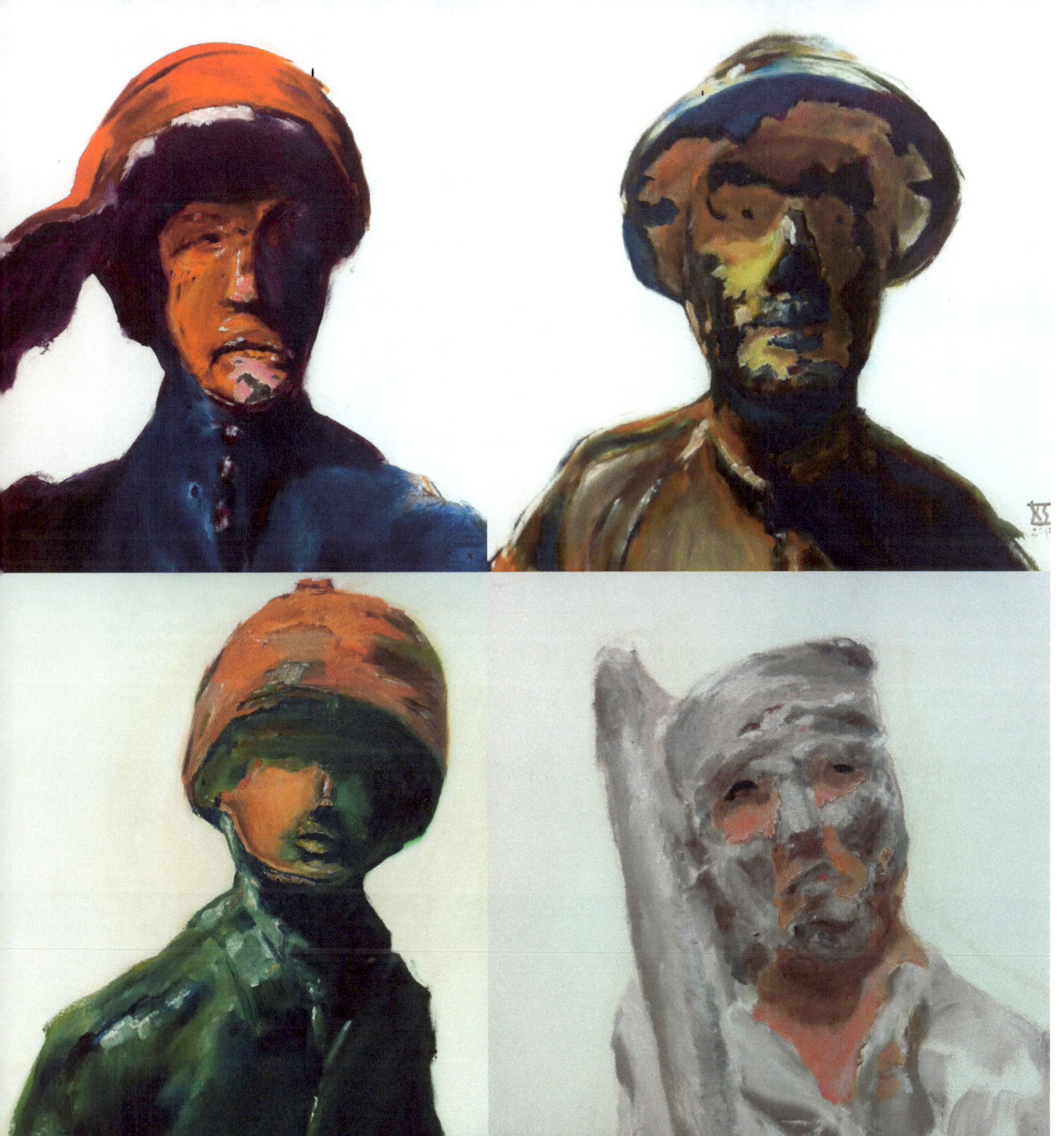

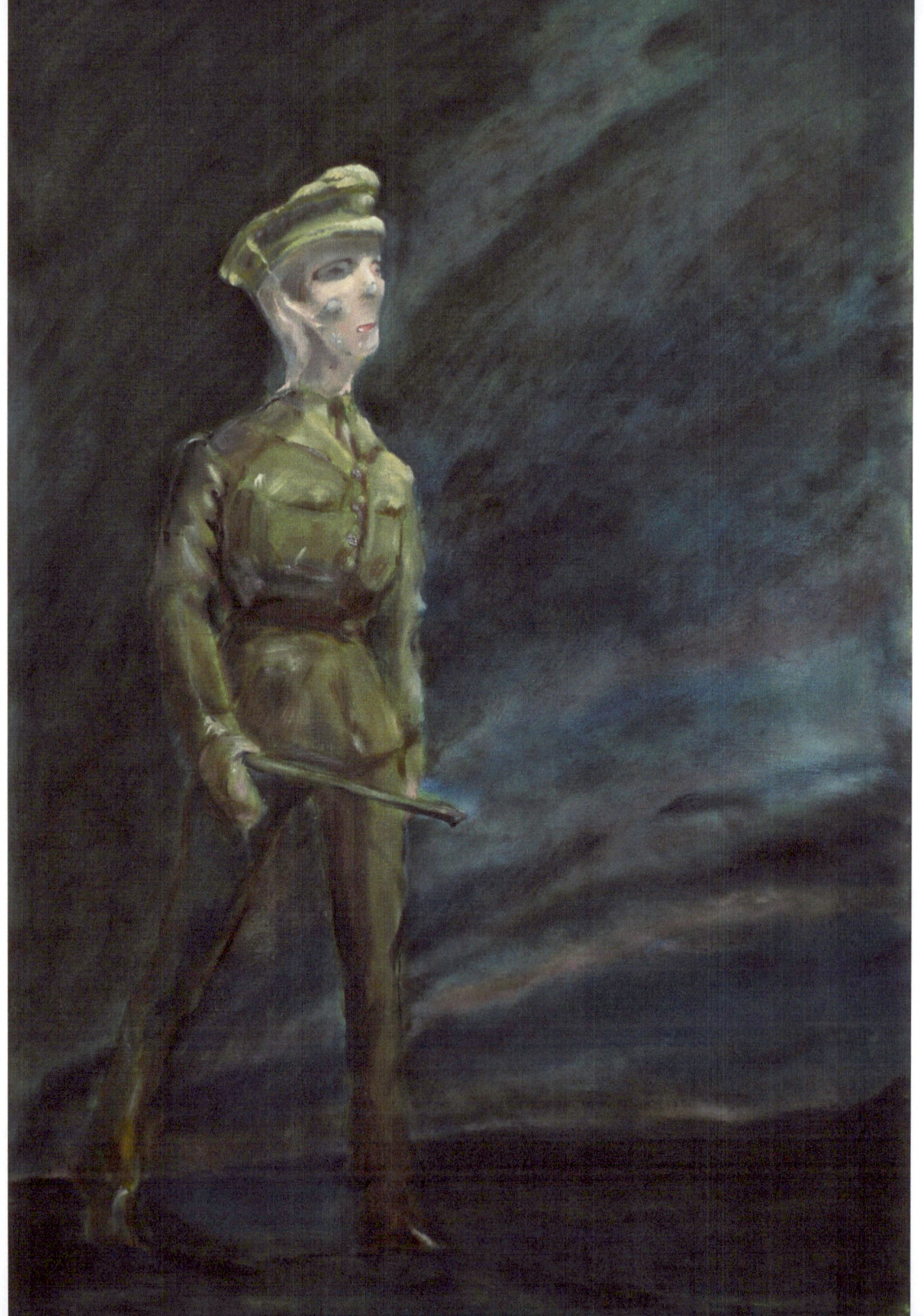

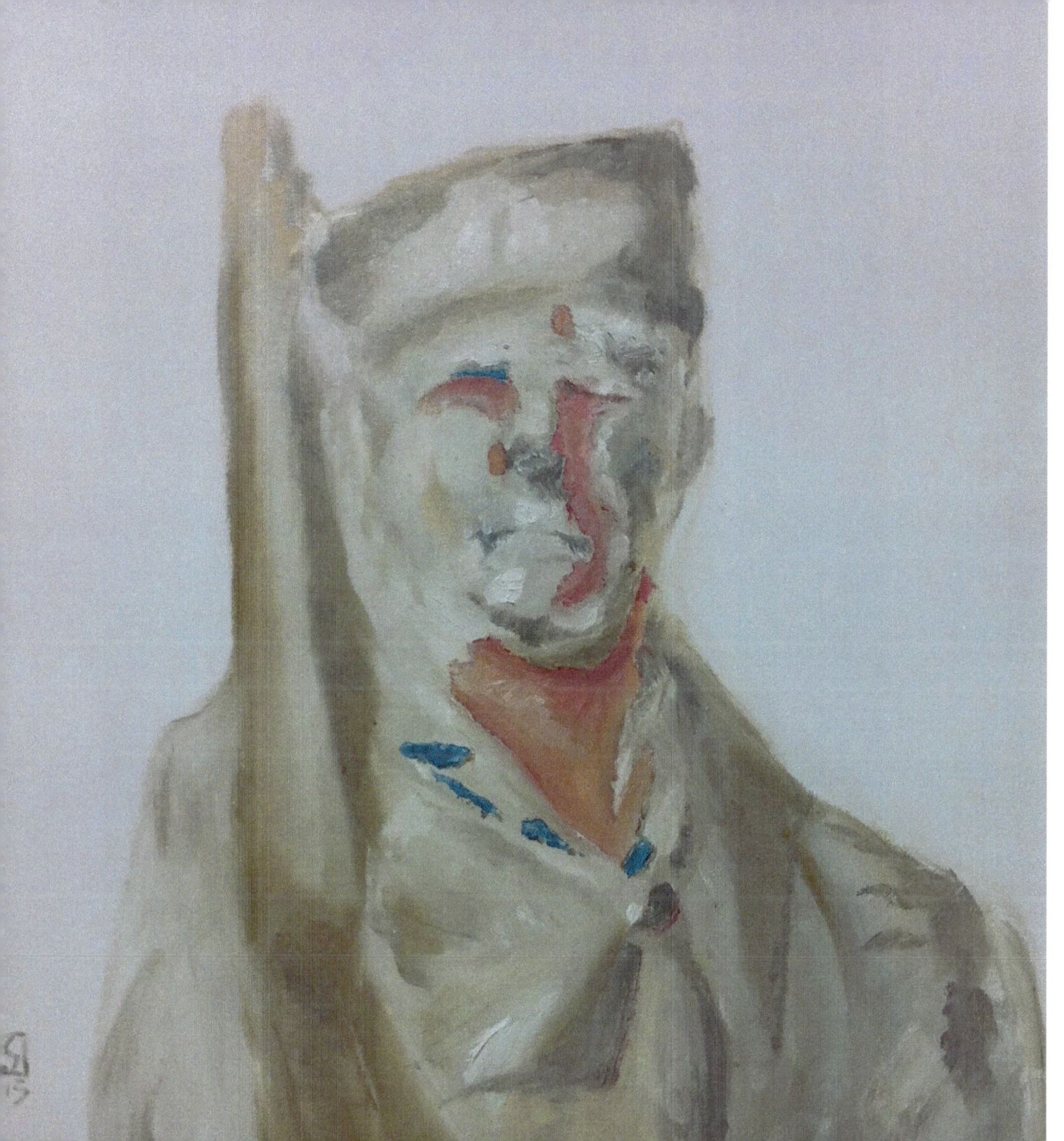

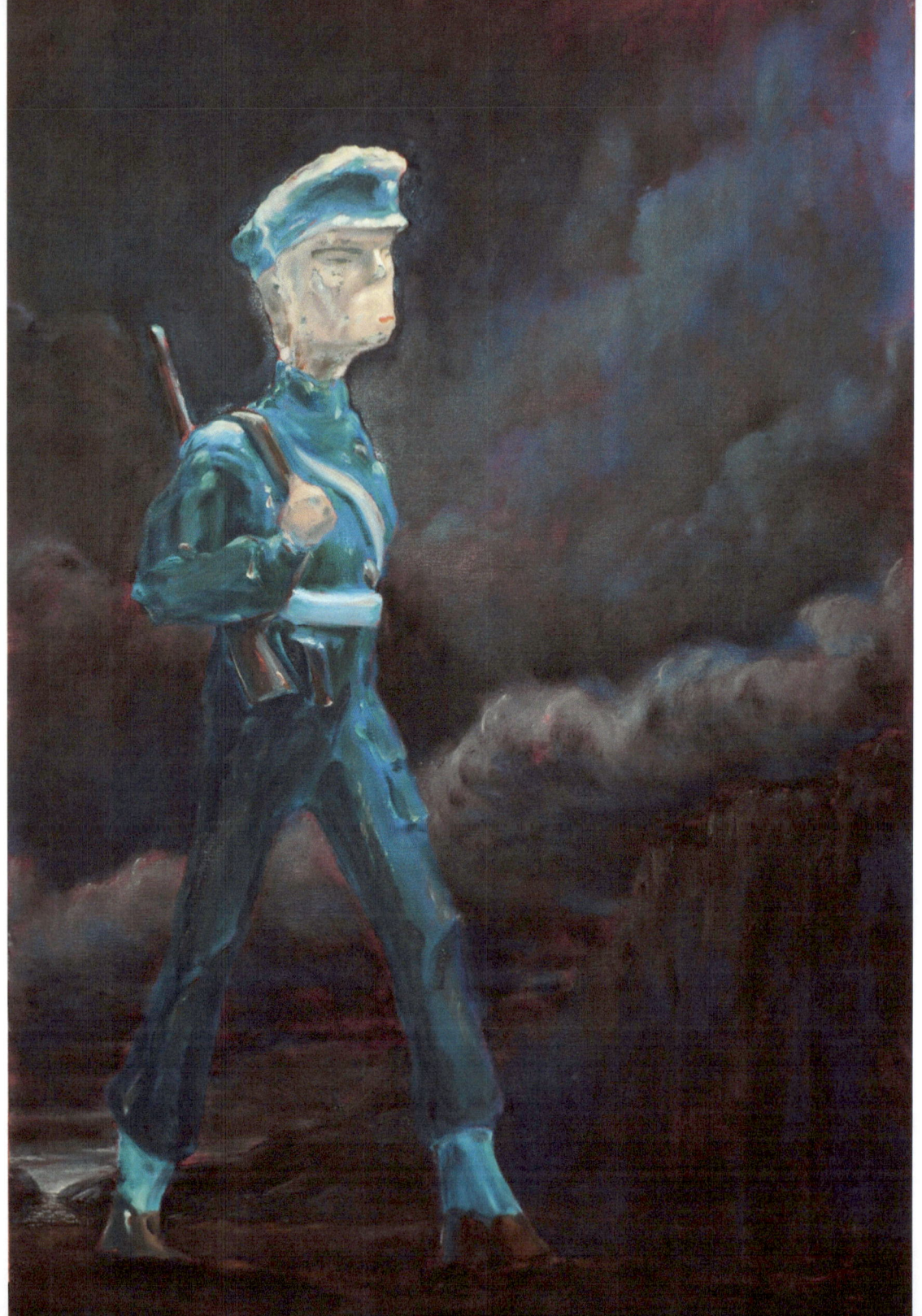

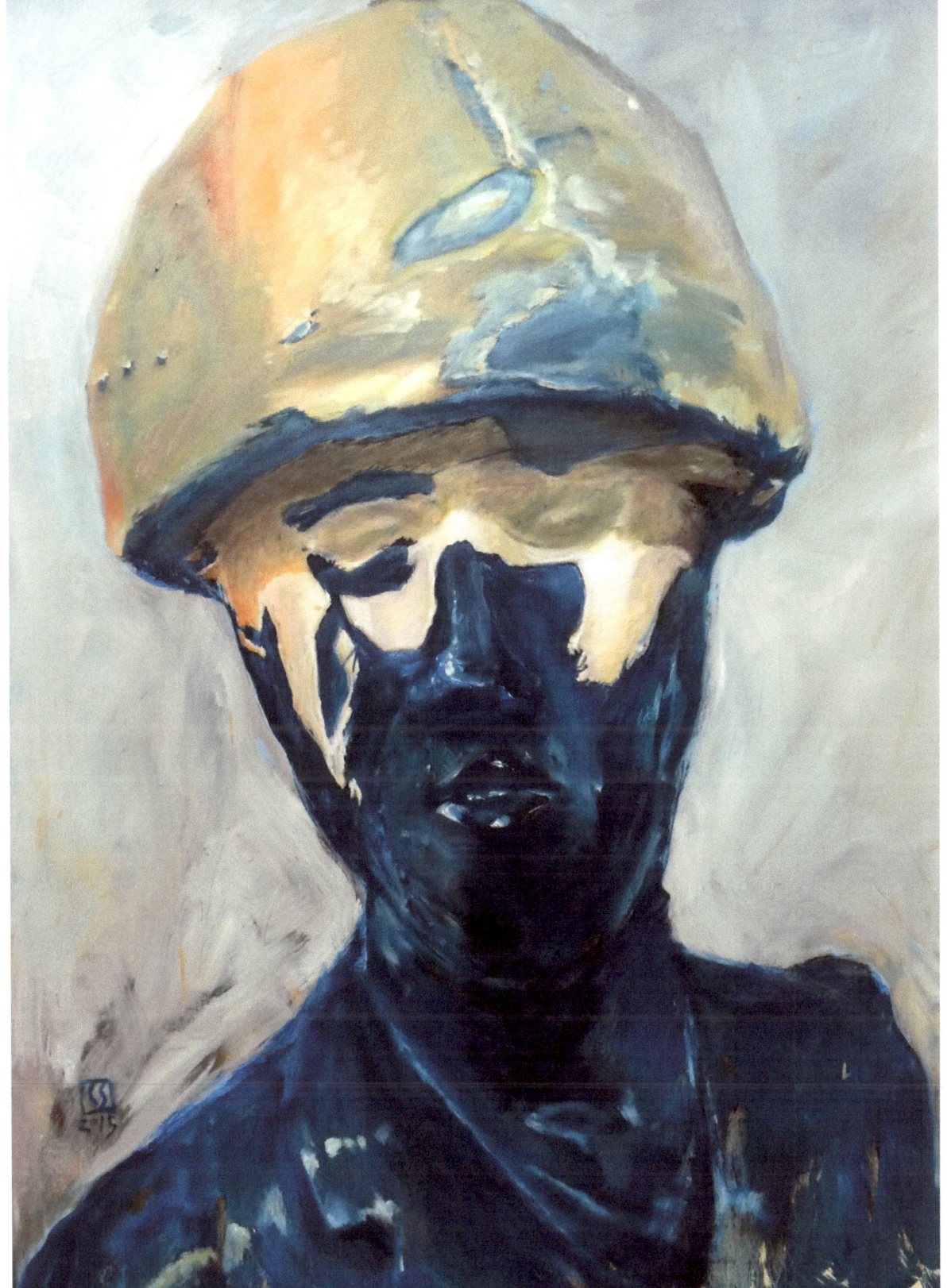

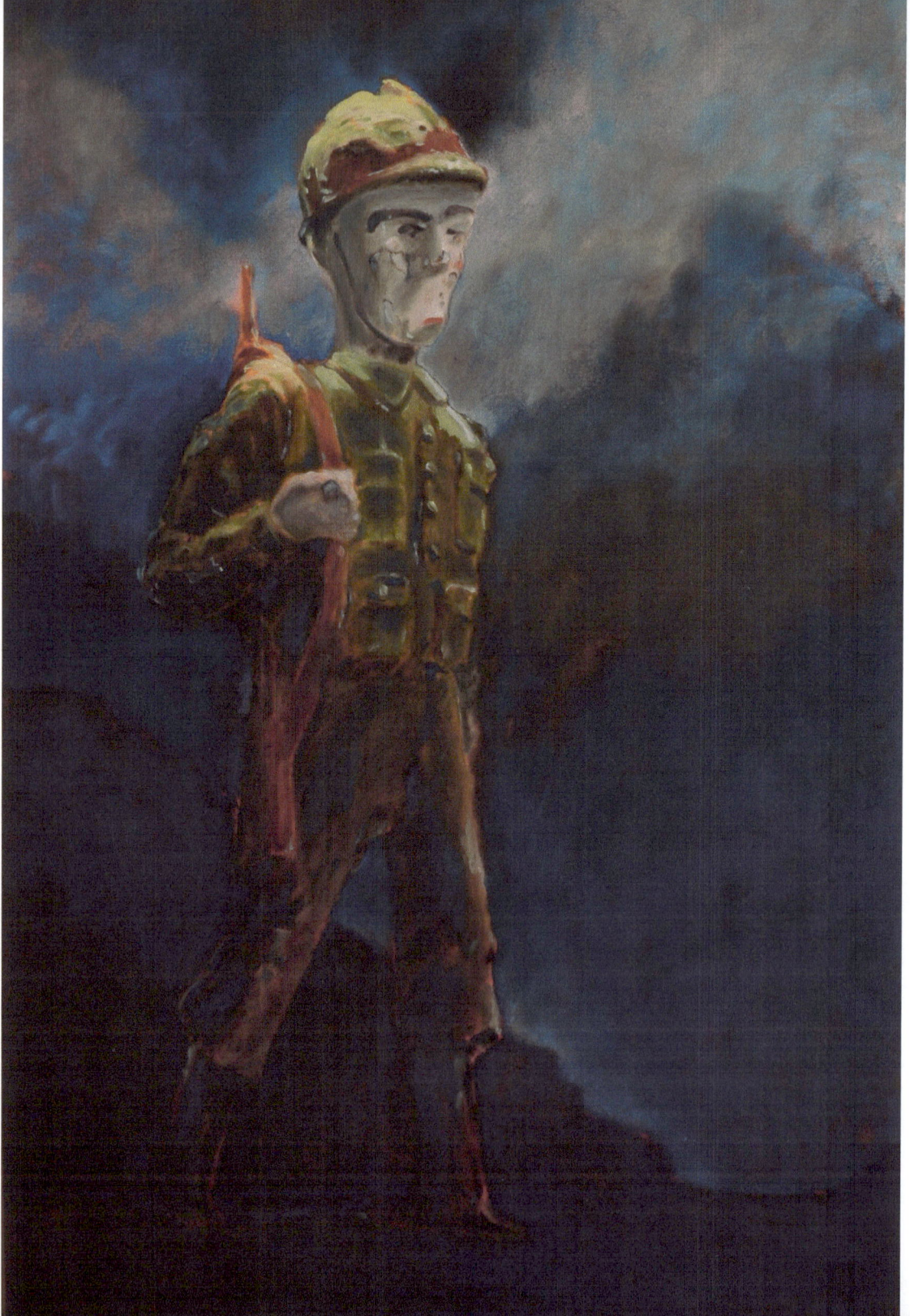

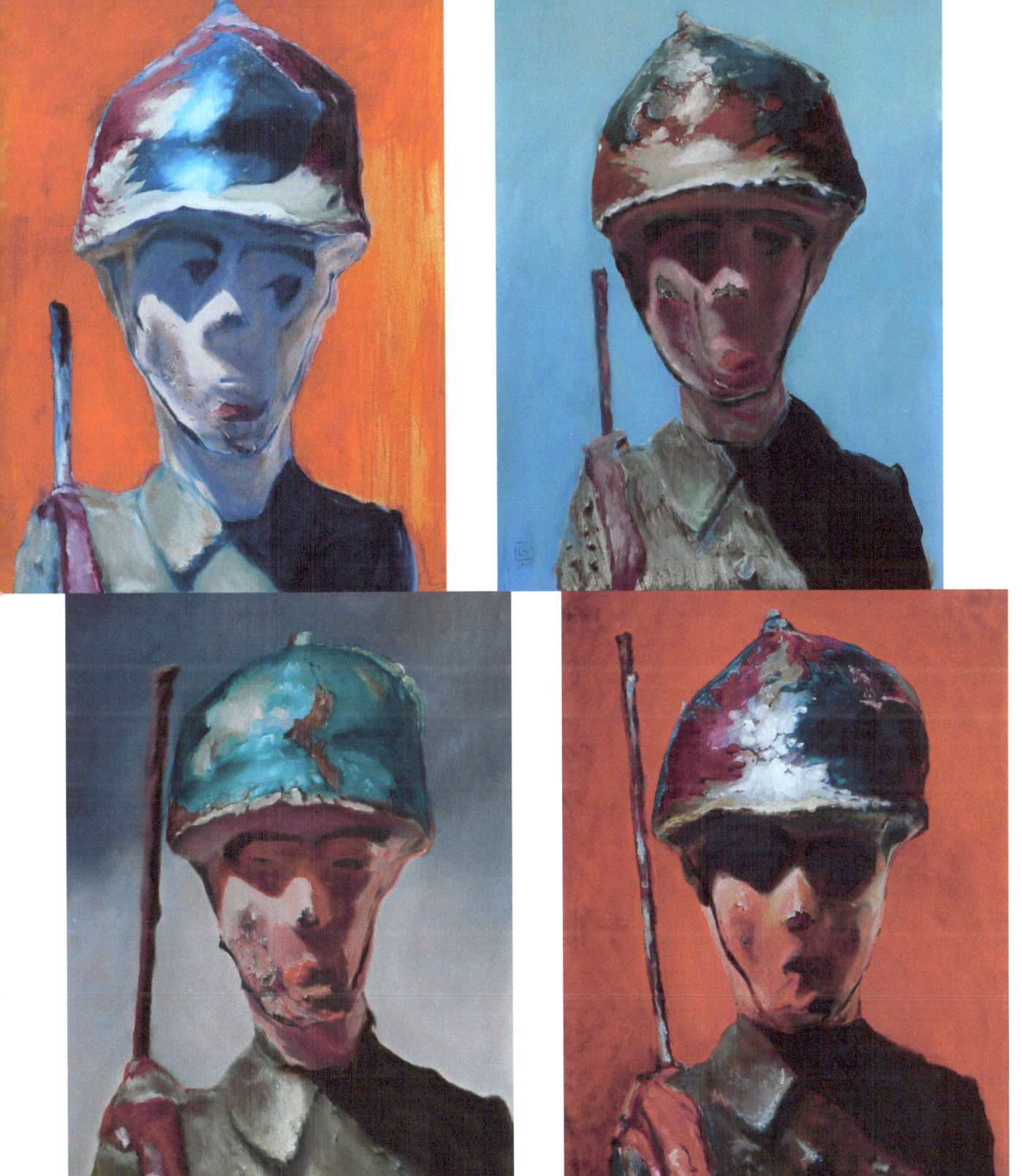

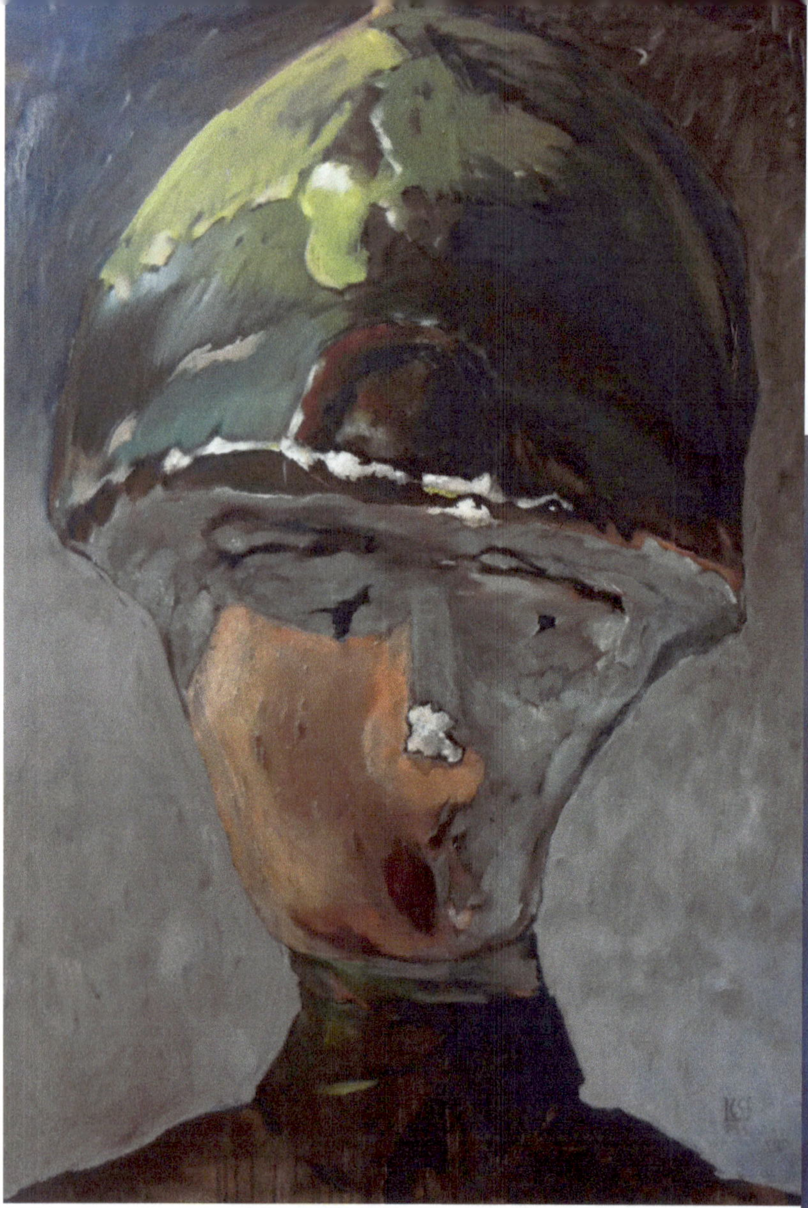

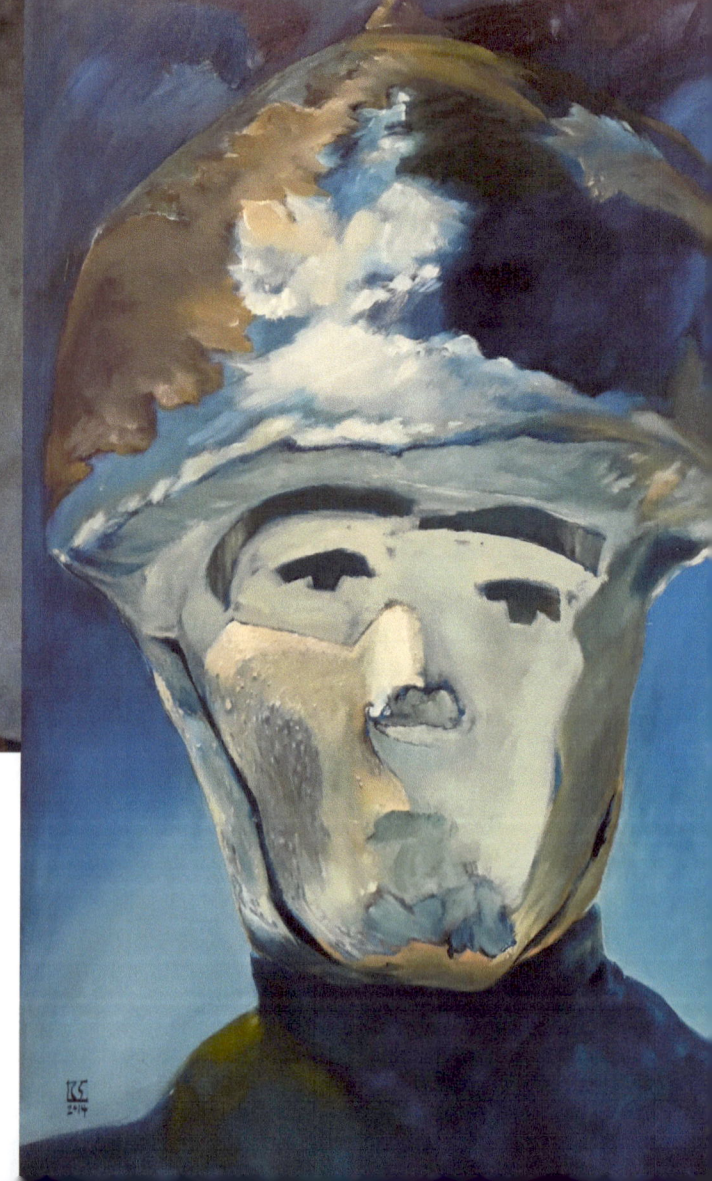

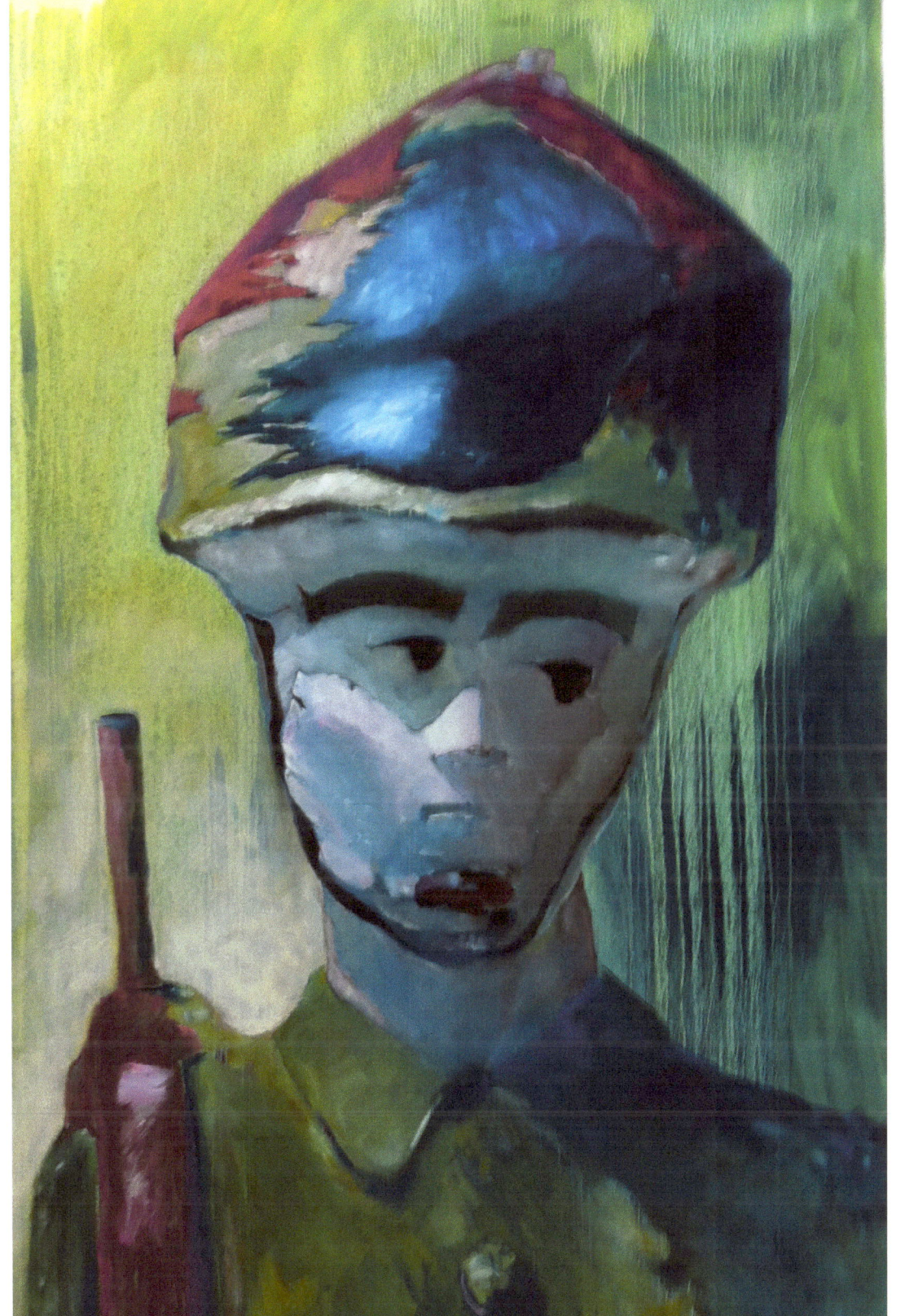

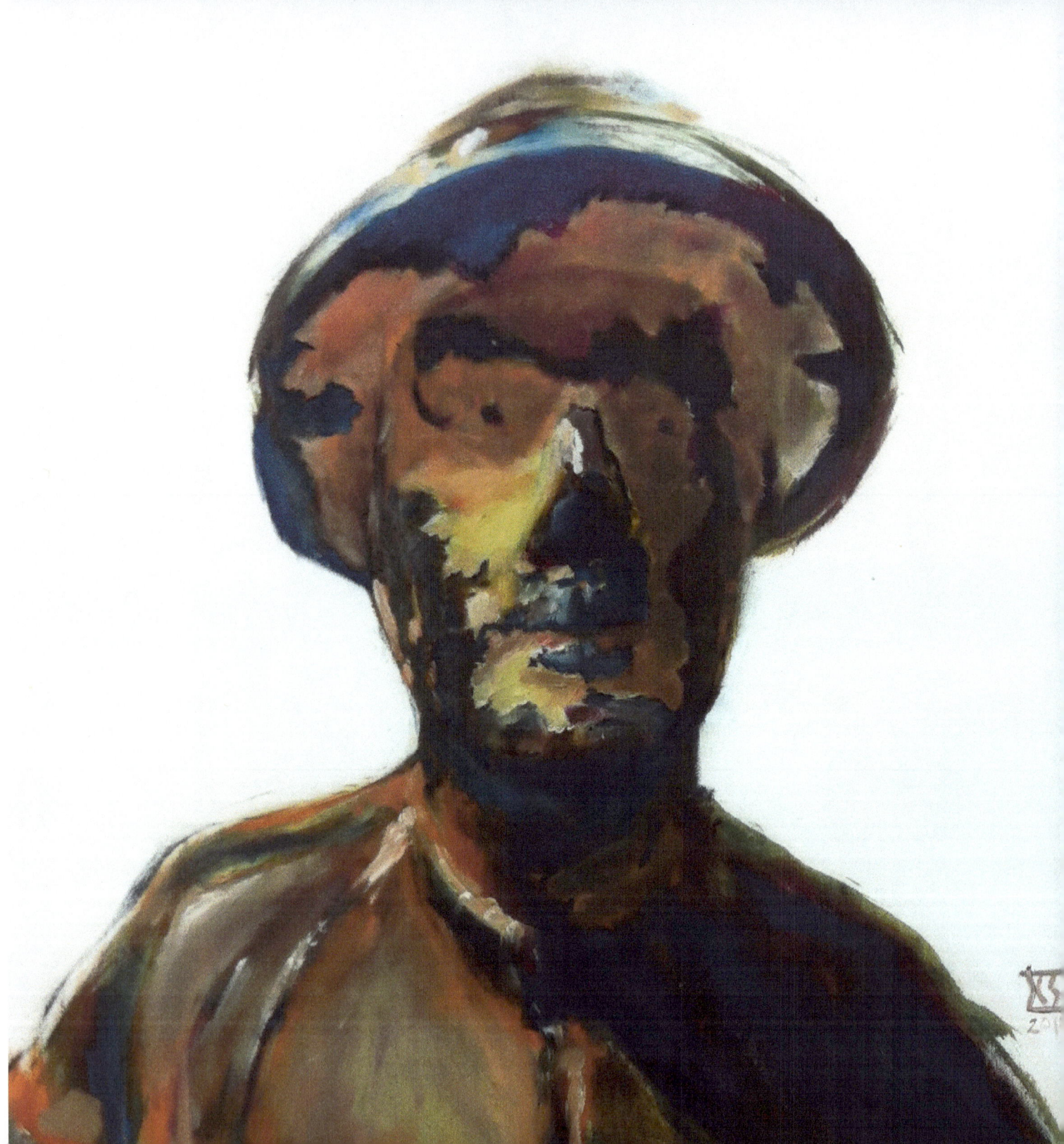

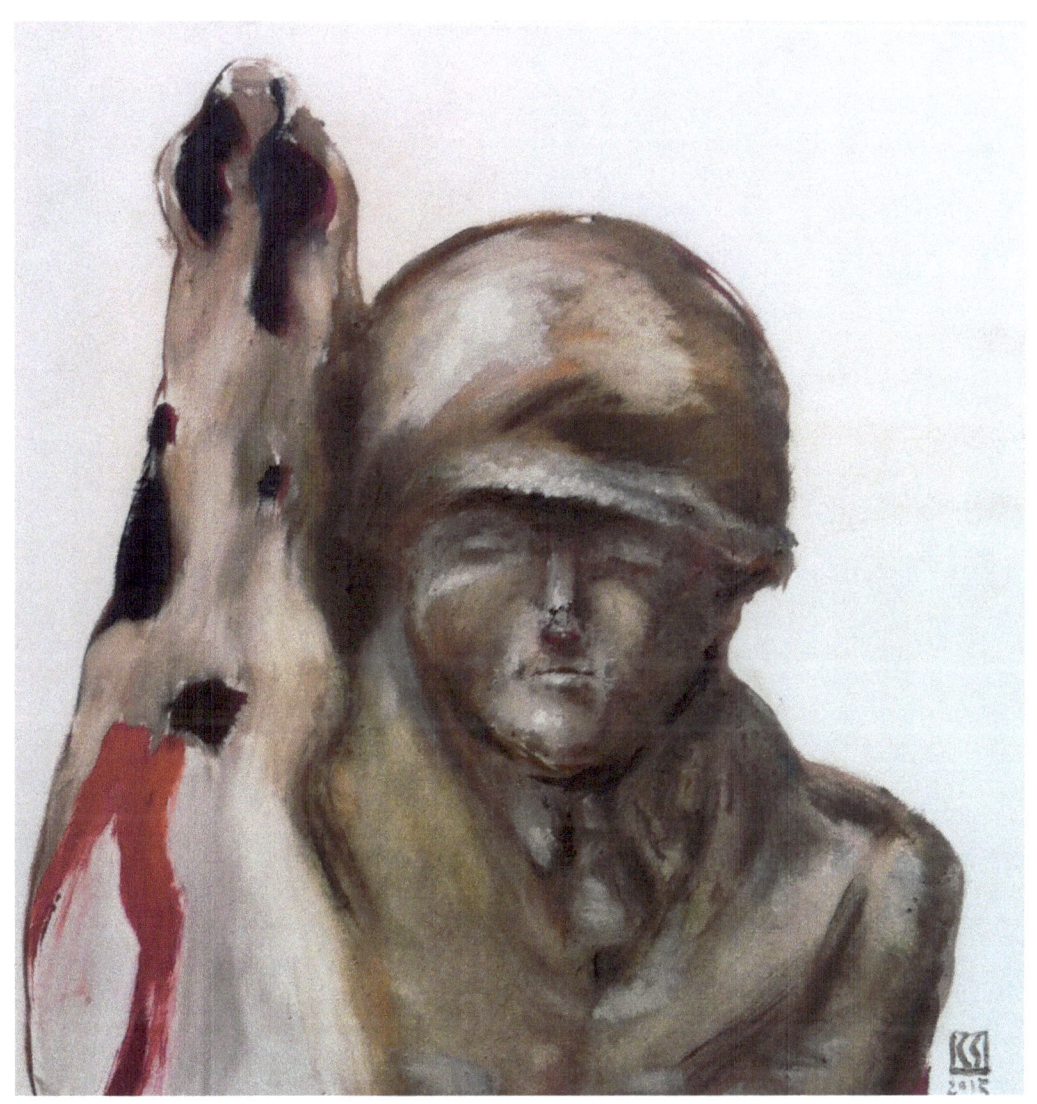

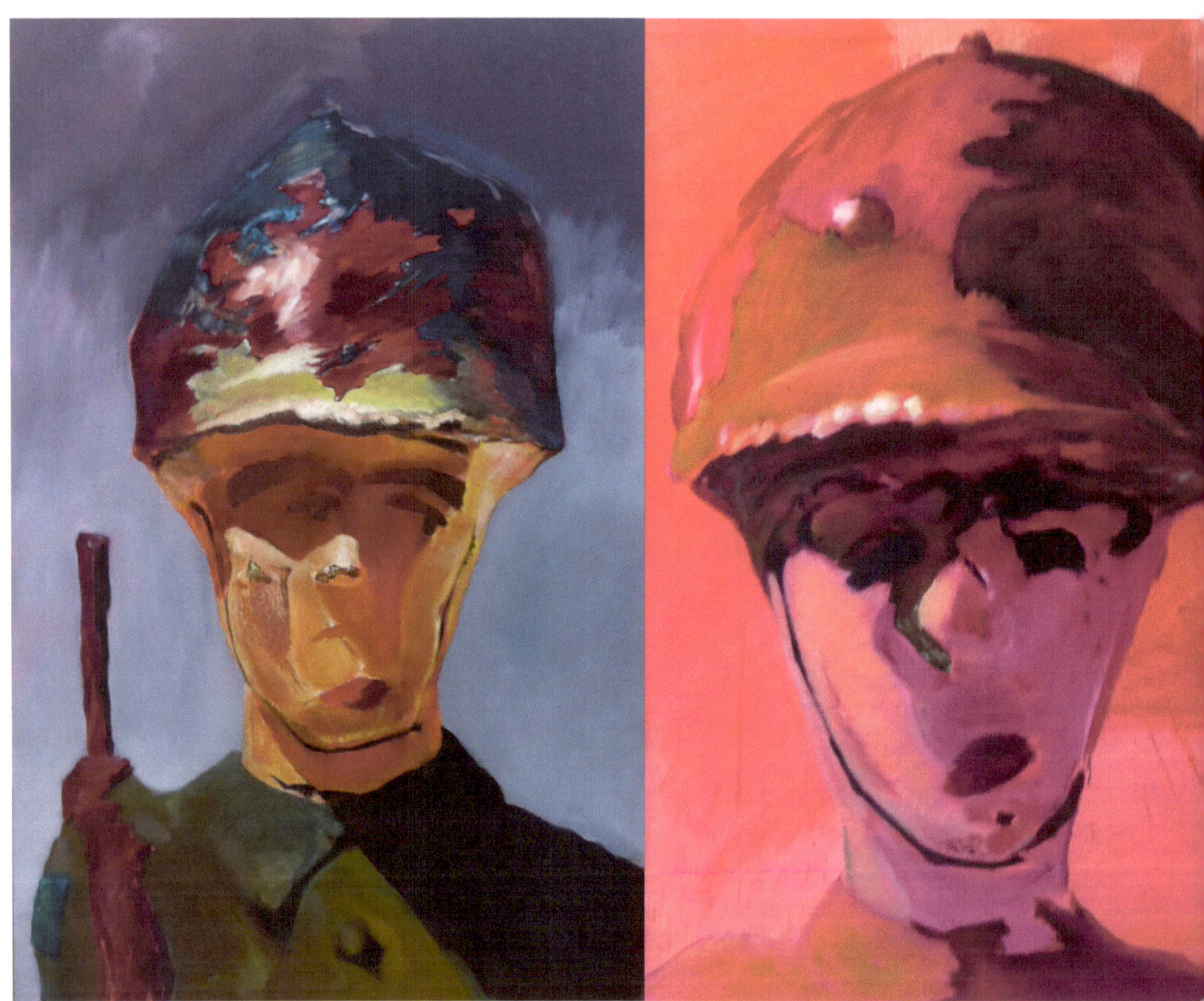

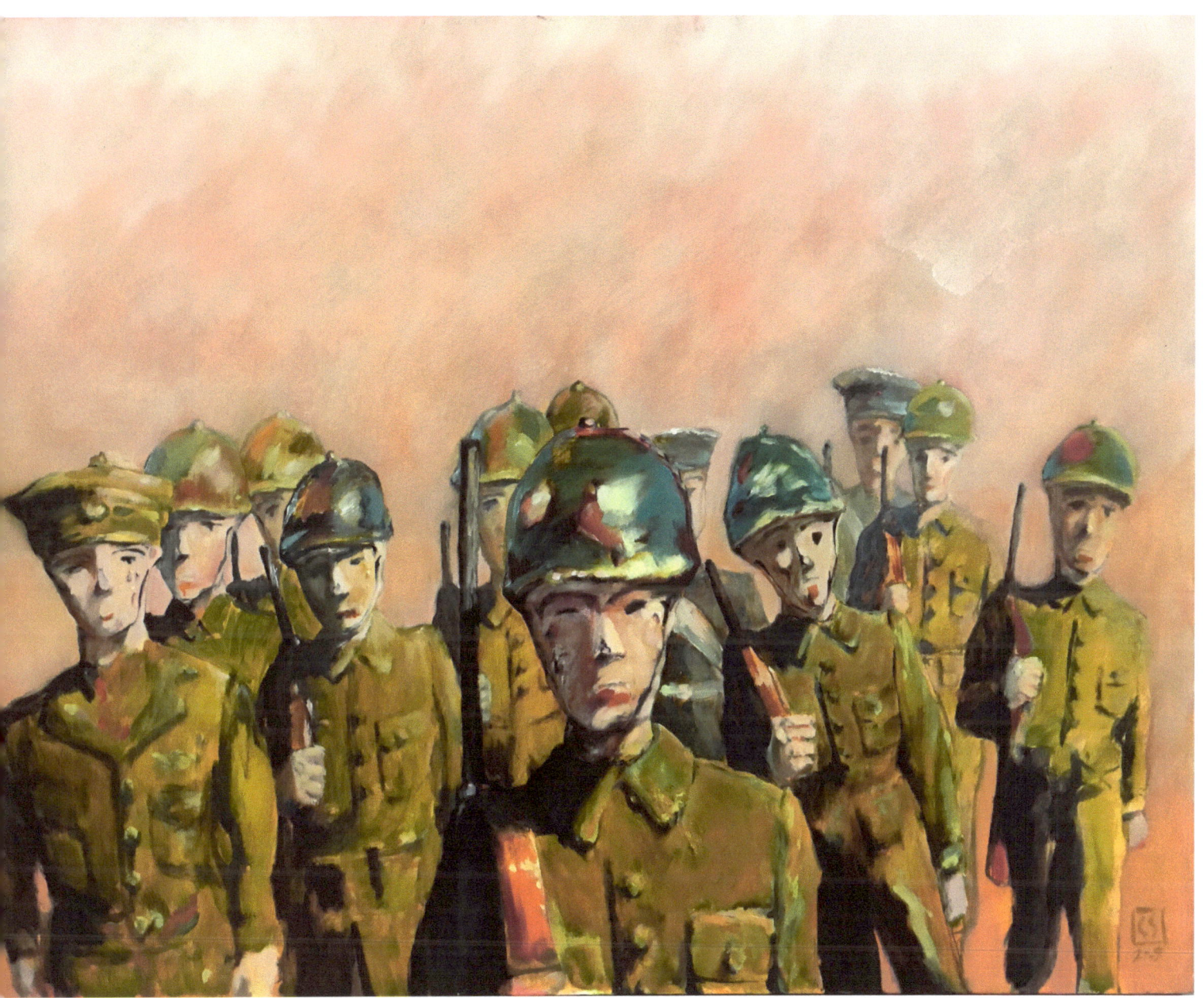

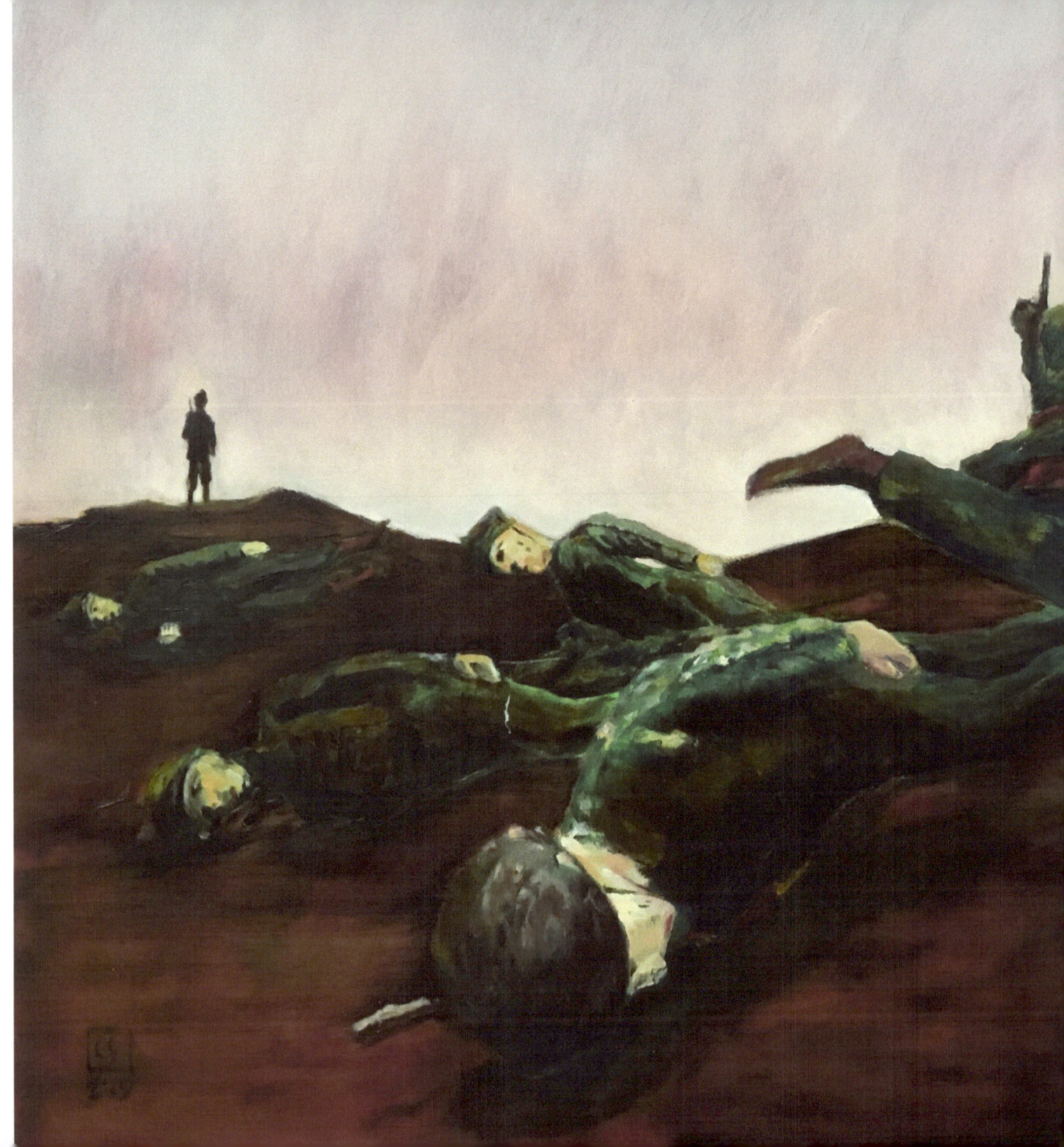

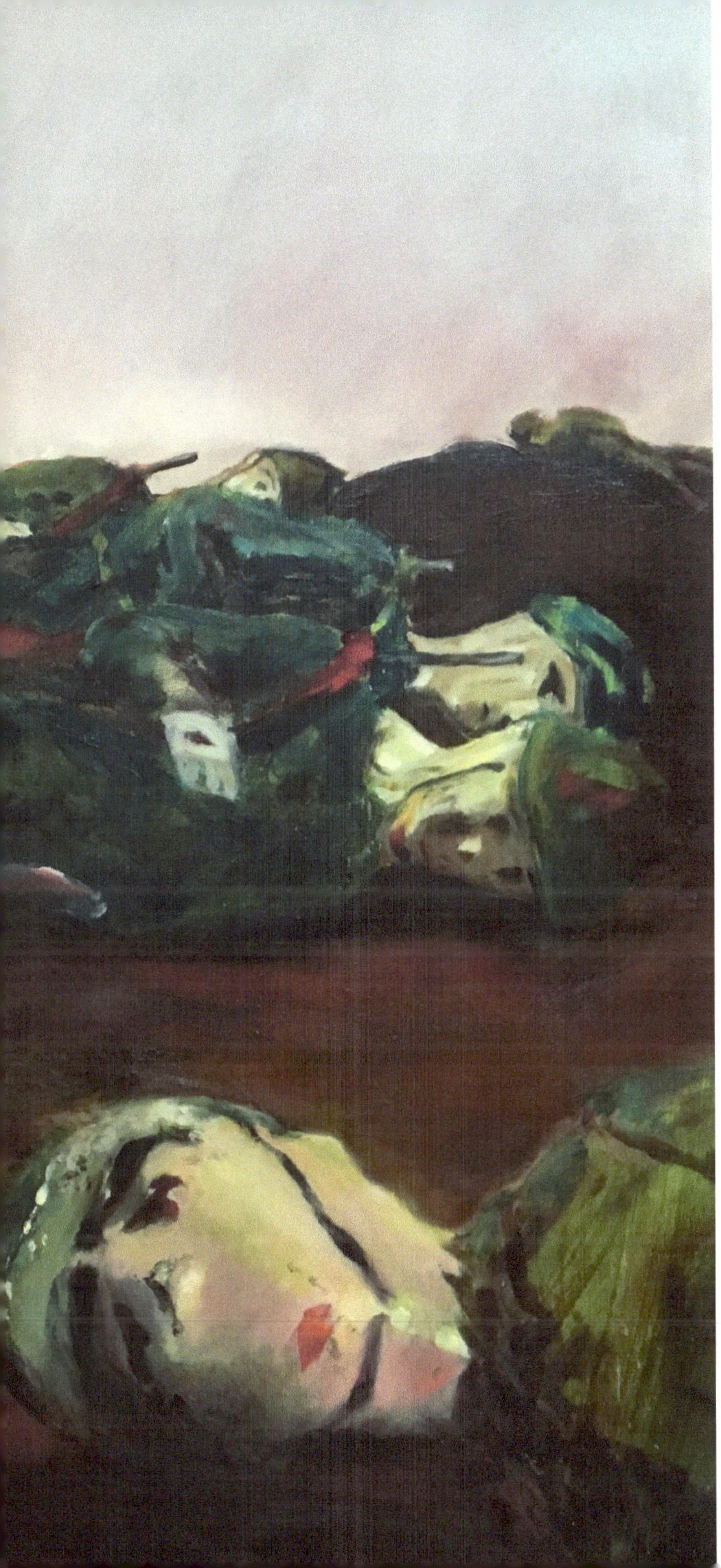

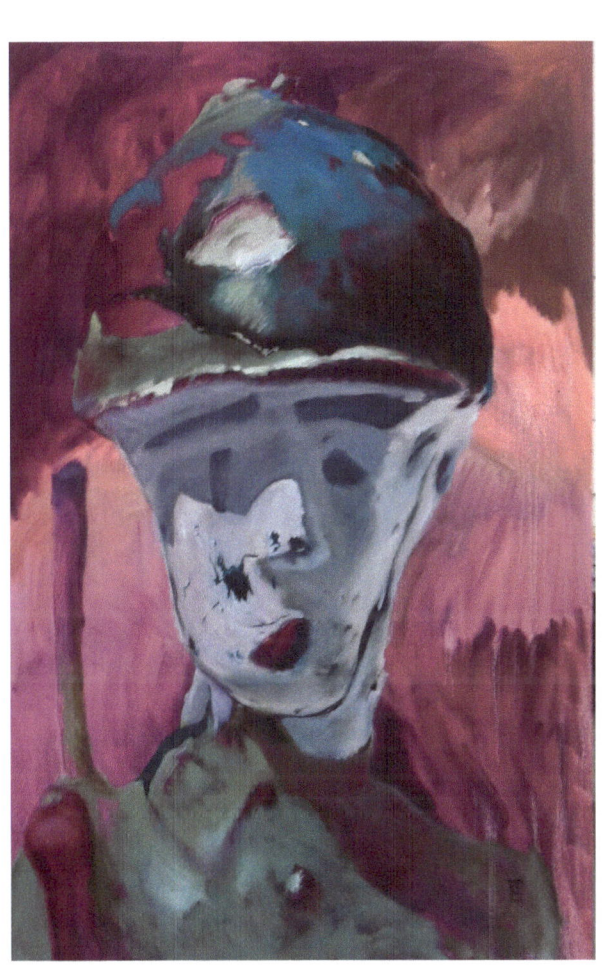

SOLDIERS

By Charles Swenson

ISBN 978-1530550722

Published by Coagula Publications
974 Chung King Road
Los Angeles, CA 90012

All paintings in this book are oil on canvas.
All drawings are mixed media on paper.
Sculptures are plastic army men and glue.

The artworks in this book date from 2007 thru 2016.
Please inquire for more information on any piece.

ALL INQUIRIES – please contact COAGULA CURATORIAL GALLERY
www. coagulacuratorial. com · 88gallery @gmail.com
1 (424) 226–2485

Book Design: Future Studio Los Angeles

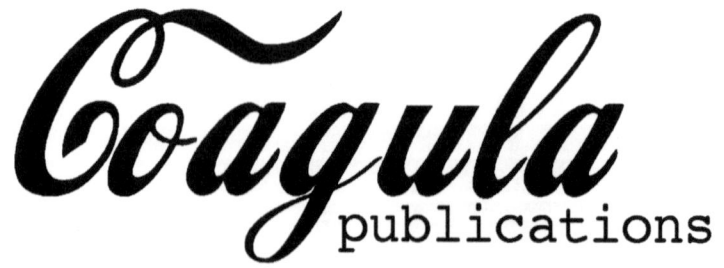

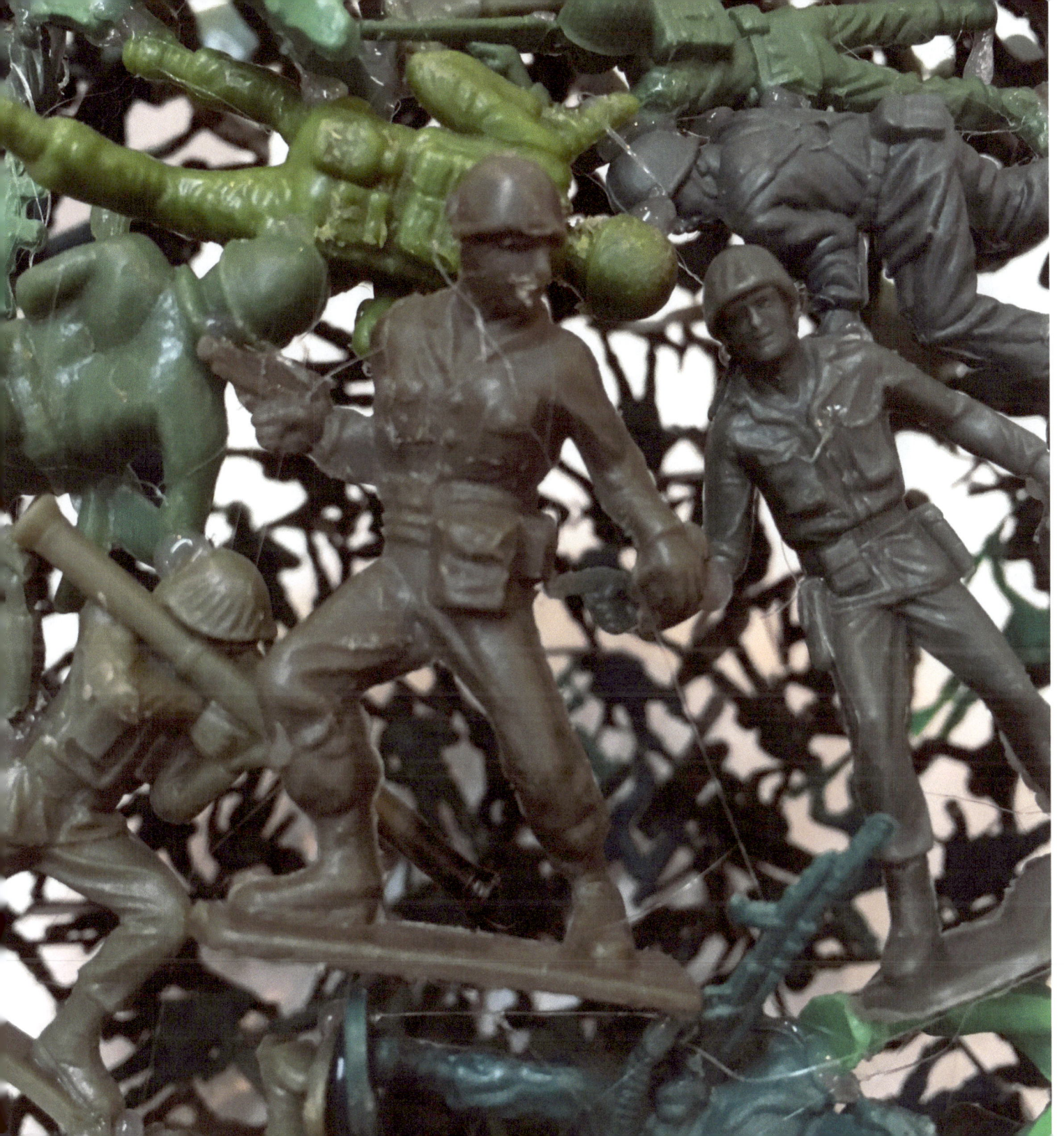

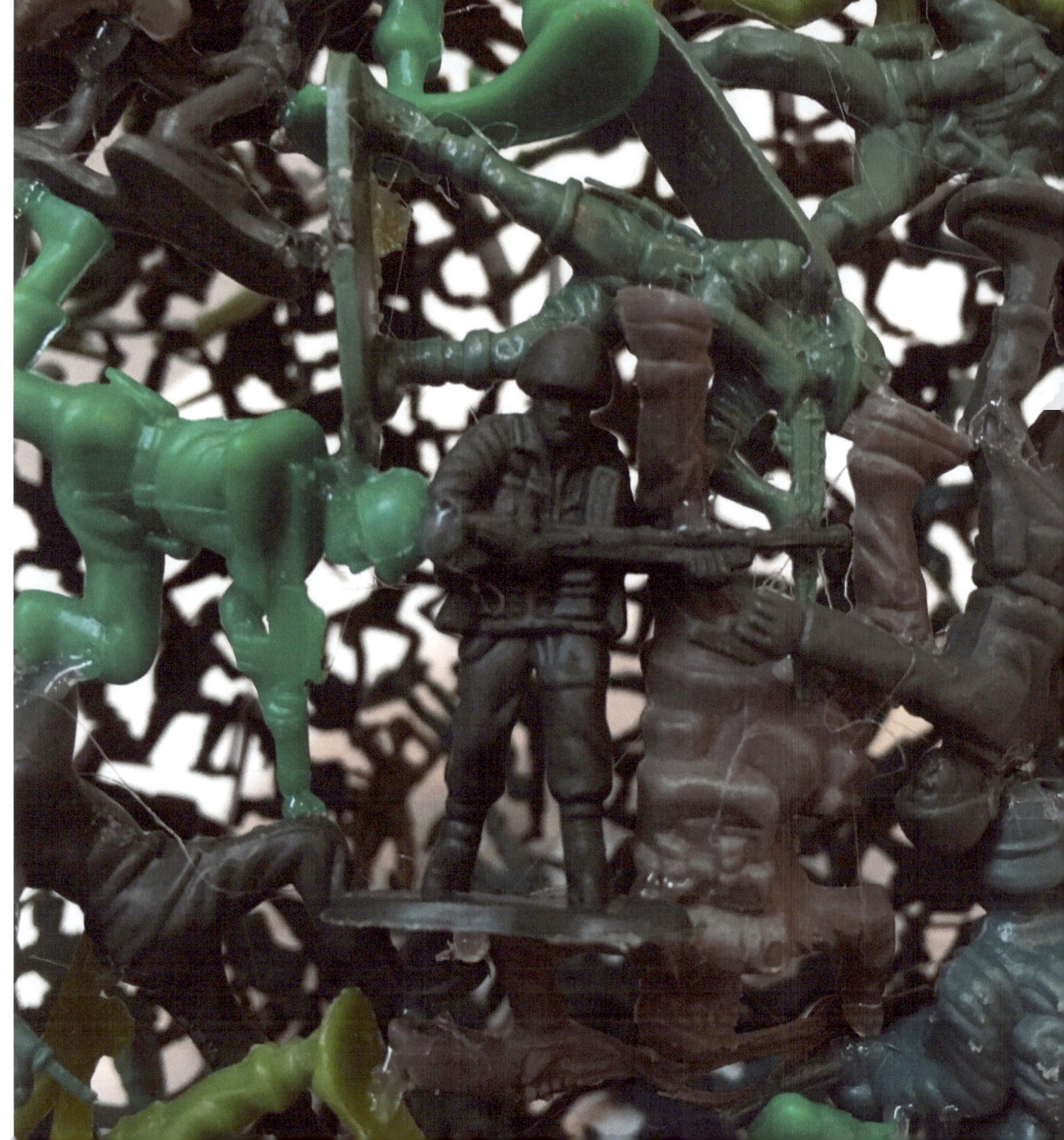